An Introduction
to Programed
Instruction

PRENTICE-HALL INTERNATIONAL, INC.

London • *Tokyo* • *Sydney* • *Paris*

PRENTICE-HALL OF CANADA, LTD.

PRENTICE-HALL DE MEXICO, S. A.

An Introduction To Programed Instruction

32547

WILLIAM A. DETERLINE
American Institute for Research

PRENTICE-HALL, INC.
Englewood Cliffs, N. J.

Third printing ....August, 1964

LIBRARY OF CONGRESS
CATALOG CARD NO.: 62-14016

PRINTED IN THE UNITED STATES OF AMERICA
49307—C

To David J. Klaus

Preface

*F*ew instructional developments in American education have attracted so much attention in so short a time as teaching machines, programed instruction, and the connotations these names immediately evoke. Since industrial training and academic education are extremely expensive, involving many millions of dollars each year, successful instruction is an absolute necessity. The uses of programed instruction are very promising for both industry and education because there is strong evidence that significant increases in efficiency, economy, and speed of instruction can be produced.

This book is about devices for the presentation of programed instruction, programs of instructional material, learning principles involved in programing, the underlying controversial issues, and the relationship of the machines, programs, and principles to existing instructional methodology. This book, a nontechnical introduction to the basic notions underlying auto-instructional methods, is designed to acquaint the reader with some of the current points of view concerning the promise and potentialities of these methods for all kinds of instructional situations, whether involving academic classrooms, industrial training courses, or independent home study programs.

There are many topics in this area which are points of active controversy between individuals concerned with the development of effective auto-instructional programs, and I have tried to avoid biasing this presentation in the direction of my own theoretical preferences. To the extent that I was not able to avoid making these preferences obvious, I apologize to those favoring opposite points of view. No final data are available at this stage of development to make clear the most appropriate techniques that should be used in the construction of programs to produce maximum learning of specific subjects by specific kinds of students. Those individuals who are directly involved in advancing this instructional methodology all agree on one point, regardless of conflicting views on program construction: the demands for effective and efficient instruction can best be met by the incorporation of auto-instructional materials into existing educational facilities. We need not only more qualified teachers, but also additional instructional techniques. Enthusiasts of this new technology feel that programed instruction will have a profound effect on education.

The orientation of this book is largely due to my association, at one time or another, with Drs. Lloyd E. Homme, Robert Glaser, Henry E. Klugh, David J. Klaus and Mr. Alex W. Andres, all of whom, along with Dr. Robert Silverman have read the manuscript and have provided me with valuable comments and suggestions. Miss Lynne E. McHugh, who edited the entire manuscript through numerous revisions and kept track of deadlines, deserves much of the credit for any clarity present in these pages. I also wish to thank the American Institute for Research for permission to reproduce the illustrations used in this book, and Dr. James G. Holland for his permission to reproduce the data which appear in Table 2. An introductory book of this sort cannot possibly refer to or recognize all of the original sources of the many ideas that have been produced in this field, and I regret the necessity of having to exclude discussion of many of the technical considerations involved in programing. Although many people in various fields of research and development have contributed to the materials and methods of programed instruction, the original contributions of Dr. Sidney L. Pressey and the influential work of Dr. B. F. Skinner have provided the foundations of research, theory, and methodology that have made auto-instruction, and this book, possible.

W.A.D.

Contents

An Introduction
to Programed
Instruction

1

Introduction

Human aspirations and ideals are intimately related to human emotions. The emotional attitudes of approval and disapproval in a given culture are usually expressed through certain words. It is often difficult to disentangle the attitudes expressed by those words from their descriptive meaning. Since the Industrial Revolution a continuing complaint has been heard that the use of machines has led to the debasement and the materialism of our civilization. The word "machine" has thereby acquired a heavy emotional burden. The same burden is now rapidly piling up on words such as "automation." Thus the phrase "automation of education with teaching machines" represents such a summation of horrors for some people that it blocks intelligent inquiry into the merits of teaching machines. (Blyth, 1960)

If the vigor of the protests against an idea and the intensity of the enthusiasm for that idea are valid criteria of the importance of an issue, then the subject of teaching machines is one of the most important current topics in education. What is meant by the statement that a machine teaches, or for that matter, that a teacher teaches? What do they do? They do not work with passive, unresisting materials as does a painter. A painting is an inanimate object, entirely a function of the activity of the painter. Students are not inanimate objects, and the finished products of instruction are determined as much by the activity of the student in reacting to the teacher as by the activity of the teacher in providing instruction. The important event in any classroom is the activity of the student, who either learns or does not learn, and it is the responsibility of the teacher to bring about the occurrence of behavior which maximizes learning.

1

As educators we are willing to say that a teacher taught a class even though many of the students may have learned very little. We should be more rigorous and define teaching as *the performance of those activities, and the manipulation of those conditions, that produce learning*. If this definition of teaching is acceptable as a realistic statement of objectives and results, then the question, "What does a teacher do?" can easily be answered: a teacher arranges for learning to take place. Some teachers produce greater learning in their students than other teachers, that is, some teachers are far more skillful than others at arranging the specific conditions that involve students in that behavior that is called learning. The emphasis in the classroom must always be on the behavior of the students and on the various ways in which learning can be produced. Rousseau, as an educational theorist, specified the ideal learning situation as a tutor with only one student, for under these conditions the teacher can devote his full attention, ingenuity, and time to the instruction of his one student. He can proceed at a pace that can be modified as often as needed to suit his student, and he can provide as many examples, as much repetition, and as much active participation by the student as he desires. Obviously, this is an attractive situation for both the tutor and the student, and many teachers, faced with the daily task of trying to produce complete understanding in thirty or more students, would find a tutorial teaching assignment extremely attractive. Surely many teachers would predict that the effectiveness of their teaching would increase if they were permitted to apply all of their skill and knowledge to the instruction of only one student at a time.

Teaching machines have been compared to tutors in terms of certain key similarities in the student activity produced by a tutor and that produced by a teaching machine. The similarities are there, and can best be identified by looking closely at the tutor and the tutorial process.

A tutor possesses some knowledge or intellectual skill that he is to impart to the student confronting him. How does he go about this? You must realize that the tutor has an advantage that is denied the classroom teacher, for the tutor can check the progress of his student by engaging the student in continuous and active discourse, requiring the constant attention and unbroken participation of the student in dealing with subject matter. We learn by doing, and the tutor has the student do things: answer questions, think aloud, guess, compute, put ideas together, discuss, etc.; the tutor is always there listening, skillfully guiding, hinting, correcting, and praising success. The tutor can proceed with knowledge of his student's progress at every moment in the instructional process, and the student always knows exactly how well he is progressing. The tutor, if he

is planning ahead, might take notes on the content of the tutorial, writing down those approaches that work best, and revising his plan as the tutorial proceeds. Many of Plato's dialogues show Socrates, master tutor, at work. The most skillful performances by Socrates occur in dialogues, not monologues. The tutor engages the student in an active interplay, not a one-way transmission in which the student passively listens. The tutor instructs the student, and then the student is required to engage the tutor. Unless learning has taken place in the first step, the student is unable to engage his tutor in discourse; however, if learning has occurred in the first step, then additional learning takes place when the student actively performs. It is not so important that the tutor tells the student that the Battle of Hastings was fought in 1066. What matters is whether or not the student can tell the tutor—or anyone else—when the Battle of Hastings was fought, and this is the objective of instruction: to have the student display and act upon knowledge that he obtained during the instructional period.

So the tutor goes on, following this procedure of imparting information and quizzing the student, gradually developing the desired level of mastery of the material. As he does this the tutor should take careful notes, evaluating his own approach and its effectiveness, with an eye to later revision of his presentation so that it will be even more effective with his next student. If the tutor has performed this careful recording of effectiveness and carefully revises his program of instruction, he may find, after using and improving his guide a few times, that he has developed so skillful a sequence that he need only read it, step by step, allowing the student to respond appropriately, then continuing to the progressively more complex expression of knowledge by the student. After a time the tutor may feel that his tutoring sequence, which by now has been extensively tested and revised, is self-contained to a point where the tutor's presence is not even required; the entire tutorial program may be reproduced so that the student reads it, writes his responses to each step, and proceeds through the highly effective program all by himself.

Of course, more than one set of the materials can be produced, and the personal attention of the tutorial presentation can be given to many students all at one time. The tutor is always available when a student needs him for any reason, but much of the tutor's routine work has been lifted from him and he is more readily available to more students more of the time. Also, the tutor is able to deal with all of his students at much higher levels of discourse, since the fundamentals are being taught by his carefully sequenced program, which keeps the students actively engaged, carefully guided, appropriately corrected or praised, and permits each student to proceed at his own, self-determined rate of speed. The program not only gives information and requires a demonstration of understanding by the student, it also includes a method of indicating the correctness or incorrectness of each response by the student, for no misconceptions should be allowed to slip through.

The tutor, if he is interested in mechanical gadgetry, might develop a device that will present the program, step by step, to the student, and he might, if he is a whimsical sort, call his device a teaching machine. He knows, and we know, that the machine doesn't really teach a thing; the tutor, not the machine, is the teacher, and all that the machine does is present his program to the students. The effectiveness of instruction depends entirely upon the characteristics of the program that the tutor has devised. If the program effectively directs the behavior of the student, and appropriately manipulates the conditions under which the student makes his responses, learning will take place.

Programs of this sort do exist, as do devices used for their presentation, and although "teaching machines" was at one time the most popular title for this field of interest, *auto-instruction* is now much more widely and appropriately used as a name for this educational technique. Other commonly used labels include *programed learning, self-tutoring materials,* and *automated instruction*. Auto-instruction does not refer to every kind of correspondence or home-study course, nor to all other kinds of teacherless instruction. A truly auto-instructional program provides the basis for a very close interaction between the student and the subject matter, because the program involves the student in active manipulation of the material in a sequence that has been developed through actual trials and revisions as the program was constructed. Perhaps *programed learning* or *programed instruction* include the necessary connotations to distinguish this very special kind of individual instruction from other less rigorously conducted individual course work. The identifying characteristic of an auto-instructional program, whether presented by a teaching machine or some sort of specially constructed book, is the active role assigned the student. Other characteristics of auto-instruction include logically sequenced small steps systematically moving to specified goals, immediate knowledge of progress for the student, and self-pacing by the student. In addition, an auto-instructional program is tested and retested by having students use the program. After each use, the program is revised and modified on the basis of the students' responses and achievement. Only after the program has undergone thorough and rigorous testing and revision can we be confident that the program accomplishes its objectives. An ordinary book may well proceed in small steps, and may include periodic exercises or examinations which provide knowledge of results or progress—and certainly a student reads a book at his own pace—but unless it provides careful guidance and continued active responding by the student, it does not represent the teaching machine program, or auto-instructional approach to learning. By active responding we do not mean the overt mechanical activities demanded by teaching machines and their programs, activities such as writing words, pushing buttons, turning knobs or dials, or turning pages; these are largely irrelevant activities necessary only for the student to progress through the program. Active responding means thinking, verbalizing at an intellectual level, and reacting to the subject matter. A program, unlike a book, does not simply present material to a student and then leave it up to the student to learn—or fail to learn. A program carries a student through a specific series of steps that lead him progressively closer to the terminal objectives toward which the program was written.

The responsibility for instruction lies with the program so that less of the burden of learning falls upon the student. An auto-instructional program accepts this responsibility, and is written in such a way that the desired terminal behavior, that is, the knowledge or skill that the program is designed to impart, is developed in a systematic fashion. One of the first programs to become commercially available, a college algebra program, went so far as to guarantee that any student who used the program would receive a passing grade in the course, or the cost of the program would be refunded. Subject matter presentation that leaves learning to chance by placing the responsibility for learning on the student could not systematically produce learning on a money-back guarantee basis!

Audio-visual devices such as television, motion pictures, and tape recordings have become extensively used in American schools at all age and grade levels, and most educators are becoming convinced that these tools can assist the teacher by efficiently presenting subject matter to the students. To a limited degree audio-visual devices perform part of the teacher's job; to a much larger degree they only supplement the activities of the teacher. A television lecture replaces part of the teacher's discussion of a given topic, but additional coverage of the same topic is usually necessary. The full extent of the usefulness of audio-visual materials and their most effective methods of application have not yet been fully determined, but undoubtedly accessories of this sort are finding a permanent place in most schools. Auto-instructional materials can also serve as accessory and supplementary teaching aids, but auto-instruction implies several unique characteristics which distinguish it from devices which simply present subject matter. The most significant difference between an aid such as a motion picture and an auto-instructional device is in the amount of responding systematically called for on the part of the student, and in the fact that a student has no control over the rate of presentation of most audio-visual material, but controls completely an auto-instructional program presentation. It is possible to respond actively to a motion picture and to learn from it; unfortunately it is also possible to observe it passively and uncomprehendingly. A student is less likely to learn from any kind of stimulation, including films, books, and lectures, when his role is primarily a passive one.

There is nothing mysterious or unusual about the principles underlying auto-instructional methods. The Socratic method of producing learning by making students respond actively to questions and by guiding their discovery of the answers is not a new idea in education; many teachers use this method as much as they are able. It is an exciting method of teaching, exciting both for the students and for the teacher. Mass education severely restricts this personal interaction between teacher and student. The oft-voiced objection that auto-instruction might dehumanize education is simply not valid. The demands of mass education have done this to a significant degree, and one of the attractive features of auto-instruction is its potential ability to provide mass instruction in a highly personalized manner. A student using a teaching machine interacts with a non-human mechanical device, but he also interacts, and to a much greater and more personal extent, with the person who prepared the conceptual material that the machine contains.

A teacher is only as good as her effect on her students; the same is true of a machine and the material it presents. A teaching machine may relieve a teacher of a large part of her teaching responsibilities, but few advocates of auto-instruction would suggest that teachers are to be replaced by student-operated instructional devices. The human teacher is far more versatile and adaptable than the most effective teaching machine, and these characteristics will always be essential in the classroom, for students need the personal, intellectual stimulation that the informal tutorial or seminar provides. As we shall see later, the roles of the teacher may be changed and improved markedly by the advent of auto-instruction, since many of the least desirable and least effective of the teacher's many activities can be incorporated into auto-instructional programs.

Auto-instruction, if it lives up to its expectations, can do much to overcome the difficulties that accompany mass education and the need for educating more students with fewer teachers. Industry also has shown a keen interest in the potentialities of auto-instruction as applied to the field of industrial training, since many millions of dollars are spent every year on recurring training expenses. Training, like education, is important and expensive. Neither can afford to be less than maximally effective. Experimental, theoretical, and methodological articles concerning programs and program construction have appeared by the hundreds since 1958 when the auto-instructional field began to mushroom, and most of the programs available at the end of 1960 were still in the experimental phase of their development. During 1961 dozens of effective and comprehensive programs appeared, and the publishers of both the Encyclopedia Americana and the Encyclopedia Britannica had embarked on the development of large-scale programing projects. Exploratory studies have been conducted and experimental programs have been developed in standard school and college subjects of all kinds, and in such not-so-standard topics as electronics for junior high school students, quinary numbers for first graders, electrocardiogram reading for medical technicians, and the English money system for American tourists.

There are many different styles of programs, all of which, because of the emphasis on student involvement, seem to offer advantages for education. Much of the research that must be done will be done by teachers using programs in such a way that the effectiveness and efficiency of a program can be clearly evaluated. A teacher may be over-skeptical or over-enthusiastic, but no teacher can afford to be disinterested. Experimental evaluations of auto-instruction are being conducted throughout the country, with many of the experiments being performed in actual classroom situations. A broad sample of these experiments and their results will be described in a later chapter of this book, following several chapters presenting a detailed discussion of auto-instruction methods and some theoretical considerations pertinent to any discussion of instructional technique. In the last chapter the auto-instructional approach is analyzed in terms of some of its relationships to our existing educational structure, including some of the possible implications that this technique has for students, teachers, and school administrators.

2

Pressey and Skinner

*T*he so called "teaching machine movement" is not a new development unless the stress is placed on the word movement. The first teaching machine was patented in 1866, although the device did not include all of the features that present day auto-instructional devices incorporate. Sidney Pressey, a psychologist, developed a machine shortly prior to 1920 that could produce measurable amounts of learning in students, but after experimenting and publishing his results, he found little enthusiasm among either educators or psychologists.

Pressey's machines were essentially multiple choice testing devices (See Figure 1). They differed from pencil-and-paper tests in that the student was informed of the correctness or incorrectness of each answer as soon as it was given. A question appeared in a small window in the front of the machine along with three or four possible answers to the question, and the student selected an answer from those listed by pressing a corresponding button. If he pressed the correct button a new question appeared; if he pressed an incorrect button the question remained in the window, an error was tallied on a counter, and the student had to try again. The machine adequately performed its testing function, but what is more important is that students learned to discriminate between right and wrong

9

answers by using the machines, and that they were able to transfer their knowledge to other questions dealing with similar principles. Pressey believed that the use of devices of this sort could produce significant changes in the effectiveness of instruction, but in 1932 he wrote,

> The writer has found from bitter experience that one person alone can accomplish relatively little, and he is regretfully dropping further work on these problems. But he hopes that enough may have been done to stimulate other workers, that this fascinating field may be developed. (Pressey, 1932; see pp. 47–51 in Lumsdaine & Glaser, 1960)

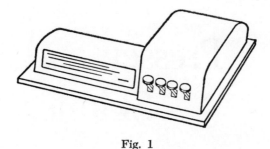

Fig. 1

Courtesy of American Institute for Research

The impetus that was lacking in the 1920's was ultimately developed by B. F. Skinner, an experimental psychologist who is primarily responsible for the current industry and interest in teaching machines. Skinner (1958) attributes the lack of enthusiasm for Pressey's machines to cultural inertia and the inadequacy of the principles of learning as they were understood in the 1920's. According to Skinner, Pressey and his associates had to work against a background of research and theory in the psychology of learning that was not adequate. This is not to say that psychologists now completely understand the learning processes, but the importance of the concept of learning as one of the cores of psychology has resulted in the development of many effective laboratory techniques for the study of learning both in humans and in less complex organisms. The conditions under which learning does or does not occur are better understood and are more readily defined now than they were forty years ago. It was partly as a result of his extensive research experience that Skinner was able to apply the laboratory methods of producing learning to the development of a teaching machine very different from that developed by Pressey over forty years before.

Reinforcement and the Classroom

In 1954, in a paper entitled, "The Science of Learning and the Art of Teaching," Skinner described the laboratory techniques that reliably produce modifications in the behavior of experimental subjects. He discussed in detail the characteristics and principles involved, and described their direct application to classroom learning and classroom teaching. Like Pressey, Skinner had a machine, and although it differed from Pressey's in most of its characteristics, it was similar in one basic respect: the student was told immediately by the machine whether each response was correct or incorrect. This characteristic is present in every auto-instructional program, whether the program is designed for use in a machine or for some other form of presentation. Although there are many other kinds of mechanical and non-mechanical devices, many different kinds of auto-instructional formats, and even different theories of how and why the materials function, the one common feature of all of these different approaches to classroom technology is the immediate feedback given the student. Organisms learn by acting on their environment and being acted upon in turn by the consequences of their actions. Certain consequences strengthen behavior, that is, increase the probability that the same response will occur again in the presence of the same stimuli. A consequence of this sort is called reinforcement, and many psychologists feel that reinforcement is the basis for all learned modifications of behavior. Receiving a material reward or achieving a goal is reinforcing, but the concept of reinforcement is much broader than the concept of rewards, since humans are reinforced by many events that do not involve material rewards. A pat on the back, a nod of approval, or simply being told, "That's right"; all of these can reinforce human behavior, making specific behaviors more likely to be produced in the future. Behavior develops, is strengthened and maintained, or is modified depending upon the kinds of consequences the behavior produces. Reinforcement might also be called "feedback" or "knowledge of results." Whatever it is called, reinforcement *works*, influencing behavior in the classroom, in the laboratory, and in the world at large.

After describing the laboratory application of reinforcement and a teaching technique called "successive approximations," Skinner analyzed the classroom situation and the role of the teacher as a source of reinforcement for her students. The conclusion appears to be obvious: it is usually physically impossible for a teacher to provide every student with individual reinforcement (feedback, knowledge of correctness or incorrectness) each time it is appropriate and necessary. For one thing, the teacher is confronted with too many children, and since much of their learning takes place covertly (not vocally or otherwise discernibly) she can rarely tell when a correct response has been made, an appropriate conclusion reached, or a correct idea produced. A tutor, on the other hand, faced with only one student, can interact directly with him, provide the guidance necessary to allow the student to arrive at a correct response, and then provide reinforcement—if the student makes overt responses so that the tutor can tell when reinforcement should be given. The tutor is in the position of being able to provide necessary reinforcement and to adapt to the student's progress by further elaboration of ideas, repetition, changes in pace, etc. Compared to a teacher who has to deal with a heterogeneous group of students, all at the same time, the tutor is in the enviable position of being able to adjust the teaching rate to fit the student. She is continually aware of the extent of the student's understanding or misunderstanding, and she is in a position to provide both reinforcement and corrective feedback exactly when needed.

TEACHING MACHINE PROGRAMS

Skinner's examination of the limitations imposed upon a teacher by the nature of the classroom, and of the events which appear to be most conducive to learning (1954; 1958; 1960), led him to develop an auto-instructional technique consisting of direct interaction between a student and a special program of material presented by a mechanical device called a teaching machine. The combination of machine and program does not simply test knowledge assumed to have been initially acquired elsewhere by the student. Pressey's programs were originally thought of as testing and practice materials to be used upon completion of regular course study. Skinner's approach is quite different from a test-like experience. Skinner's machine was specifically designed to function as a teacher of students who have had no previous contact with the subject matter at all. Each student uses a machine, thereby coming into personal contact with the tutoring which has been written directly into the program.

Skinner comments,
> This may suggest mass production, but the effect upon each student is surprisingly like that of a private tutor . . . (a) there is a constant interchange between program and student . . . the machine induces sustained activity. (b) Like a good tutor the machine insists that a given point be thoroughly understood . . . before the student moves

on . . . (c) like a good tutor the machine presents just that material for which the student is ready . . . (d) like a skillful tutor, the machine helps the student to come up with the right answer. . . . (e) Lastly, of course, the machine, like the private tutor, reinforces the student for every correct response. . . . (Skinner, 1958, p. 971.)

These are extravagant sounding claims for a mechanical gadget and some printed material! The claims, however, are not exaggerations, since each characteristic noted by Skinner is actually present in auto-instructional learning. The more important component of the special program-machine combination is the program. The material that is to be presented to a student by a teaching machine must be carefully and painstakingly prepared; standard textbook writing cannot simply be adapted for use in a machine, no matter how elaborate the machine may be. The programing of verbal knowledge into a teaching machine format is an involved process. Programing rules and techniques so far developed were in most cases devised by Skinner or his followers. There are now other types of programs, and some of the existing points of disagreement between proponents of the various methods of program construction will be discussed in Chapters 4 and 5.

The easiest way to describe Skinner's approach to programing is to describe the various characteristics of a program constructed according to his views, and to identify the function and rationale of those characteristics. A program of material is not constructed solely on the basis of either theoretical or empirical interpretations of the learning process per se. Programing as a technology has its roots in the laboratory research of experimental psychologists, but is specifically designed for practical classroom use. (The relationships between auto-instruction and experimental studies of learning are discussed in Chapter 3.) The initial step in writing a program is the specification of the terminal objectives of the course through a thorough analysis of its content, that is, the preparation of an outline which describes in detail every principle, definition, and relationship that the student is to carry away with him. Each idea must be carefully defined, along with all of its subsidiary concepts, examples, and related principles.

This first step in programing is extremely difficult and laborious, and even experienced, skilled teachers and training experts are often surprised to find that they cannot sit down and dash off a complete and concise summary of *every single fact* that a course is supposed to present to the student. Along with this specification of course content an analysis of prior student knowledge is also necessary, since the program can build only upon the things the student already knows.

Programing often requires the cooperation of several experts. The programer, who is the expert on the construction of program sequences, must have the assistance of a teacher with experience in teaching students of the appropriate ability level, and technical assistance from a subject matter expert. During the development of the program itself, the subject matter expert evaluates the technical accuracy and adequacy of topic coverage. When the objectives of the course and the outline of the ideas to be taught lie before the programer, he must then attempt to develop the most systematic order of presentation of the subject matter. Assistance in determining the order of presentation might come from the subject matter expert or from textbooks on the subject being programed, but often the programer finds that a particular sequence is used in a textbook only because the subject matter has traditionally been taught in that sequence. He may discover a more workable sequence while he is writing the program.

THE STRUCTURE OF A PROGRAM

A program consists of a series of small units, called "frames." Each frame is based on knowledge already possessed by the student, and each frame adds a very small increment to this knowledge, moving the student steadily toward the terminal behavior called "knowledge of the subject." Subject matter must be presented to a student in small amounts. If he is bombarded with too many new ideas, each briefly and all at one time, it is unlikely that he will comprehend and later be able to apply any of the concepts. A frame ordinarily introduces only one concept at a time, along with an identifying characteristic or partial definition of it. Then, in subsequent frames, the concept is built up, examples are given, and the student gradually acquires all of the responses that are a necessary part of understanding that concept. Each frame is short in terms of the amount of learning it produces, and in the actual number of words composing it. Ideally, a frame should not be more than twenty to thirty words long, although some frames must necessarily be longer. Each frame contains one or more blanks to be filled in by the student in sentence-completion fashion. The blank in a frame calls for a response that the student is able to make either because he learned how to make it in previous frames, or because it is made possible by the frame currently confronting him. The student reads each frame and then fills in the blanks; he learns by reading the frame, but it is not assumed that he is going to learn and retain the material in a frame *simply* because he reads it. The type of reading required by a frame insures active and continuous manipulation of the ideas described in the frame. As far as psychologists know, reading of this sort results in learning, while passive reading, without active manipulation of the ideas that make up the subject matter, results in little if any learning. (Thinking, of course, is one type of active manipulation. The critical requirement apparently is that the student become actively involved with the material.)

After making a response, the student manipulates the handle or knob on the machine so as to expose the correct answer, which until this time has been hidden from him. When he compares his answer with the correct answer he is reinforced if his answer is right, and corrected if his answer is wrong. He then moves on to the next frame. As mentioned before, his correct response to a particular frame is made possible by the presence of certain specific aspects of the frame. For example:

1. A teaching machine presents specially constructed material, called a program, to a student. The special material presented by a teaching machine is called a _____.

2. A teaching machine itself is not as important as the _____ that it presents to the student.

Frame one is a simple copying frame; its objective is to get the student to respond with the word *program* in the presence of the terms *special material* and *teaching machine*. The student is easily able to make the response in frame one, and this prepares him for making the same response in a slightly different context in frame two. He cannot copy the word *program* in frame two; he must remember it from his use of the word as a response in frame one. In addition to the utilization of simple copying frames, another possible way of increasing the probability that a word will be correctly produced the first time it is called for is to use it as a stimulus word in the proper context in many frames just preceding the frame in which it is first required as a response. Again, however, one of the best ways to insure that the student will make the response correctly is to have a technical word copied the first time it is called for. This may seem like a small point to belabor, but programs must be built in such a way that the student is carefully guided, step by step. Each frame seems easy, but adds a bit more to the student's knowledge and requires him to make a response that is just a bit more complex than his preceding responses.

A student learns to respond to stimuli; and stimuli that are present when a response is made become related to that response. Once a student is able to respond with the word *program* when given the stimulus phrase *teaching machine,* the programer is then able to expand the term into a concept. The program does not simply tell a student about stimulus and response relationships, it builds the relationships into the student by requiring him to state the relationship himself. The program provides all the guidance that is necessary so that the student gradually becomes capable of expressing complete relationships without assistance. Telling the student about ideas does not guarantee that learning of those ideas will take place, so a program puts the student to work using the words and concepts rather than just telling him about them and hoping that he'll learn them. A response is not called for simply to have the student practice it, and to have it reinforced. The important thing is to have it practiced in the presence of those words, phrases, and collateral or subsidiary concepts that are eventually to be able to produce the response overtly or covertly in the student. The concept of reinforcement and its role in the learning process can be developed in as few as five, or as many as several hundred frames, depending upon the degree of understanding desired. A single concept may be described in frame after frame, but each frame is written in a different form using a different example, a different form of response, and a wide range of contexts in order to broaden and strengthen the range of the student's understanding.

Both repetition and variation are necessary in a program to guarantee breadth of understanding, retention, and sustained interest, but each frame must be a little different from every other frame or the repetition becomes monotonous and the student loses interest. A frame that would appear after all of the components of the answer have been taught might read:

> A student should be reinforced immediately when he makes a correct response because _____
> _____.

The answer is to be in the student's own words. He has never been given the question in this form before, but if the preceding frames have adequately prepared him by having him learn about reinforcement he should be able to produce a satisfactory answer. This kind of program does not stress, or even promote, rote memorization. Each time the student makes a correct response and is reinforced for it, his understanding of the subject matter is increased a small, but significant amount.

The series of frames that appears in Table 1 illustrates many features of this type of program. There is a great deal of repetition throughout these eight frames. A total of thirteen responses are called for, four of them requiring more than one word. The related words, *conductor* and *conduct,*

FRAME SEQUENCE

TABLE 1

1. A conductor will carry electric current. A wire or any substance that will carry or conduct an electric current is called a _____.

   conductor

2. A copper wire will conduct or carry an electric current because copper wire is a good _____.

   conductor

3. A conductor is a substance that will carry or _____ an electric current. Rubber is not a conductor, so rubber will not _____ an _____.

   conduct
   conduct
   electric current

4. An insulator will not conduct an electric _____. Rubber is a good _____ because it will _____ _____.

   (complete)

   current
   insulator
   not conduct
   an electric
   current (or)
   not conduct
   current

5. Electric current can flow or travel along a _____, but cannot flow along an _____.

   conductor
   insulator

6. You could receive a "shock" from a copper wire unless the copper wire is surrounded by an _____.

   insulator

7. An insulator is a substance or material that will _____.

   (complete)

   not conduct
   electric
   current (or)
   not let
   current flow
   (or) stop
   current

TABLE 1—Continued

8. A conductor will ———————————————————————.
                    (complete)

                                                conduct an
                                                electric
                                                current (or)
                                                carry current

are called for eight times, five times by themselves and three times as part
of a multiple word response. *Electric current, conductor* and *insulator*
will require more development in varied contexts, and the word *flow*
will be incorporated as a response word for the first time within the next
few frames. In addition to the amount of repetition, the characteristic of
these frames most likely to appear striking to you is their simplicity. Each
frame adds only a little information, easily within the student's ability
to understand and apply correctly. The important event in the student's
contact with each frame is his responding to it so that learning can occur.
Initially the response needs to be emitted by the student in the presence
of those stimulus words that are to be tied in with the response words.
The second step is to relate the response word to many other words that
are used both as stimuli and responses. For example, the response word
current must be related to electric, flow, flow of electrons, amperes, Ohm's
law, coulomb, voltage, resistance, circuit, etc., and each of these terms
must be available as responses to the word *current* used as a stimulus,
or to any other appropriate stimulus. All of these verbal interrelationships
must be built into the program in such a way that they are directly and
adequately acquired by each student.

In order to produce a specific response early in a set of frames that are
designed to strengthen and broaden the concept identified by the response,
the programer uses "cues" of various kinds to make it easy for the student
to emit the proper word or phrase. As the concept becomes more
thoroughly learned, fewer and fewer cues are provided. In Table 1, for
example, frame number one requires that the student *copy* the term
conductor, a term which already has some meaning for most high school
students. The response *conductor* is then practiced in frame two and in
the form of *conduct* in frame three in the presence of the key stimulus
conduct current and the example *copper wire*. Because the stimulus words
electric current and *carry* have already been tied to the response word
conductor they can be thought of as key stimuli which elicit the response
conductor, thereby providing the basis for learning a relationship between

conductor, carry, flow, and *electric current.* In frames three and four the concept of *insulator* is developed initially by contrasting it with *conductor.* The sentence structure of frames three and four guides the development of the concept of insulator with rubber as an example. Through frames five and six the elaboration is continued until the complete definition in the student's own words is called for in frame eight. Here is a simple example of a frame in which the sentence structure guides the student to respond with the correct word:

> Dinosaurs no longer exist as living animals on the earth, that is, they are extinct. The passenger pigeon, like the dinosaur, is also _____.

Although a student obviously will learn something from a frame of this sort in which the answer is "handed to him" by the frame content, frames must not be over-prompted or a student may never learn to make the response in the absence of prompts. As a student acquires a progressively broader understanding of a concept, prompts and cues are gradually withdrawn until finally the student runs into frames that provide only a context or framework in which the responses must all come from the student.

> Metals are generally good conductors because metals (your own words) _____
>
> _____.

A frame like this is a "chips are down" frame. It tests not only the student, but also the effectiveness of the program. A student should face a frame of this sort only after the program has given the components with which he can unerringly produce the answer, or after the program has given him the answer itself in slightly different form. This frame is not simply a test frame, it *should* be a practice frame. There are no prompts to make the response obvious, the answer should be available to the student because of learning that has already taken place. At this point in this frame he should be able to respond correctly so that the whole answer can be further strengthened.

A "completed" program, whether it is fifty frames or five thousand frames in length, has no value whatsoever unless the programer knows through empirical tests that it produces learning in the students for whom it was designed. Programs must be tested as they are written, and then revised and rewritten and retested as often as is necessary to eliminate ambiguous frames, inadequate coverage, etc. Just as the student receives feedback from the program, the programer receives feedback from the student, who is after all the final judge and authority on the effectiveness of the program. This point is very important, and perhaps the testing that a program undergoes in the course of its development might be the characteristic that really makes auto-instruction radically different from any other kind of instructional technique. Few textbooks and even fewer lectures are developed by repeated use and revision based on a careful evaluation of the reactions of students and of the effectiveness of every phase of the presentation. A textbook may be ingenious in its structure and logical in its sequential coverage of principles, but those characteristics are of secondary importance. The relevant characteristic that must be present in any book, lecture, program, or any other method of presentation is the ability to learn. How well can a student learn from it, how quickly, and with how much effort? Programs do not arrive at their final form simply because their author believes that the frames read well and considers the sequencing to be very logical. Rather, the programs are tried out on students and are rewritten and modified as a result of each try-out, until finally the programer and his test group, working together, produce a program that is capable of accomplishing its objectives.

A program written in the style developed by Skinner and his followers has many characteristics which identify it as a Skinner-type program. First, the program consists of many small steps; secondly, the student constructs or composes answers, rather than selecting them from a limited set of answers as in multiple-choice responding; third, continual active responding is required on the part of the student after very small amounts of information have been given; fourth, reinforcement is immediate; fifth, breadth of understanding, not rote memorization, is the main objective; sixth, every effort is made to eliminate errors, the assumption being that a student most efficiently learns by being correct, not by being told that he is wrong after making an error; and seventh, the program is capable of providing for a wide range of student ability and allows each student to proceed at his own speed. The last point, which has not previously been mentioned, should also be true of most forms of auto-instruction. Although the eight frames in Table 1 seem almost ridiculously easy to you, they will not appear so to many students who might be required to use them. Skinner emphasizes the importance of a student being able to move through a program at his own self-selected rate. Faster learners, better readers, might complete a 2,000 word portion of a program in only eight or nine hours, while the slowest learner in the group might require as many as twenty or thirty hours for the same material. The point is of course that the slowest learner *can learn the material* in some finite period of time; without a program or an exceptionally skilled tutor (the latter is rarely available) the very slow student might give up and never learn, or what is probably worse, he might grind away for the same twenty or thirty hours without reaching even a minimum level of comprehension.

SKINNER'S FIRST MACHINE

A student who uses a program of this sort may have the frames presented to him by a machine, although other modes of presentation have also been developed (see Chapter 4). Regardless of the specific design of the machine—there are many research and commercial models available—all of them follow roughly the principles built into Skinner's first pilot-model shown in Figure 2. The frames are written on the disc repre-

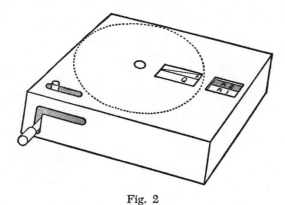

Fig. 2

Courtesy of American Institute for Research

sented by the dotted line and appear in the window marked Q. After reading the frame the student writes his response on the paper tape exposed at R^1. In using other types of machines the student may make his response directly on the blank line in the frame itself, or in a separate notebook. The student then raises the handle and the correct answer appears in window A. In some machine designs in which the student responds by writing on paper contained in the machine, as in the case of Skinner's machine, the student's answer is moved under a transparent cover (R^2) as the correct response is revealed. This prevents him from "cheating" by changing his answer. After evaluating the adequacy of his response he again manipulates the machine to produce the next frame.

The problems of machine design and construction are not difficult. Both Gilbert (1959) and Homme (1959) characterized one period in the development of auto-instruction as the year of the programless machines, when enthusiasts were devising many ingenious mechanical devices (an enjoyable task) while studiously avoiding the actual writing of programs (a much more rigorous and demanding task). Machines may turn out to be a necessary and integral part of auto-instruction, but the quality of a program, not the elegance of a machine, is the determining factor in any test of the effectiveness of auto-instructional methods. The questions of greatest importance to the future of auto-instruction are not, "Do teaching machines work?" (they do), or "Can they be of value in the classroom?" (they can), but, "How can auto-instructional methods best be used in our schools?" It is to this question that later chapters are devoted.

3

Principles of Learning

*T*he subject of this chapter is actually far more general and encompassing than its title may at first suggest, since learning, as an area or field of research and theory, means to the psychologist far more than the usual connotation of classroom or training-course consequences of instruction. It is generally agreed in behavioral science that humans are not endowed with behavior patterns of the sort that could be called instinctive behavior. Even the reflexes that come built into us are not properly called instinctive, since "instinct" is generally reserved for fairly complex patterns or sequences of behavior that appear in lower organisms without any apparent opportunities for learning having occurred. We are dependent upon learning for the development of the adaptive responses through which we act consistently and effectively upon our environment. We learn not only to read and write, walk and talk, and perform many kinds of jobs, we also learn the characteristic behavioral patterns that are called personality, character, neurotic behavior, prejudice, attitudes, and so on and on through the list of words that are used to refer to the many facets of the behavior of an individual.

Psychological theories of learning are more properly called theories of behavior, because the concept of learning is concerned with behavioral change, whether the change is in the direction of developing a new response pattern, or modifying or eliminating an already existing pattern of behavior. The role of reinforcement is emphasized throughout this book, and this emphasis parallels the concentration of attention that reinforcement has received in psychological theories of behavior and psychological experimentation during the past fifty—and particularly during the past twenty—years. The function and role of reinforcement has probably been subjected to more frequent and more rigorous study than any other principle of behavior, and although a single principle cannot account for and explain all of the wide range of differences in learned response patterns, interpretations of behavior based primarily on reinforcement theory have proven extremely useful in the explanation, analysis, and prediction of human behavior (e.g., Dollard and Miller, 1950; Skinner, 1953).

The analysis of human behavior is complex and fascinating whether in an experimental laboratory, a classroom, or simply in the world at large. Everyone to some extent indulges in the casual interpretation and explanation of his own behavior and that of others around him. Systematic laboratory research in the area of human behavior has grown and advanced in the past half-century until it has touched all of us. Psychological tests, for instance, measure various aspects of performance and are widely used for the purposes of evaluation and prediction. These tests have grown out of the systematic and scientific study of the human organism as have psychotherapy, human engineering, motivation research, selection and training procedures, and, of course, auto-instruction.

Experimental research in psychology and education as it relates to human learning is often of a practical and applied nature, immediately applicable to the classroom. Research in behavior is not, however, always specifically designed to answer a practical question or to provide a method or principle that can immediately be put to use in the world outside the laboratory. Much research is "basic research," which can be thought of as research that is designed simply to broaden human knowledge. The basic research of many physicists during the early part of the twentieth century had few immediate applications, and seemed far removed from the practical outside world, yet some of those same basic research findings have led directly to the development of electronics, the harnessing of nuclear energy, and to other rather extremely practical applications.

Although college students, who are readily available to faculty member experimenters in both education and psychology, have probably been the most popular subjects for experiments in learning, basic research in the behavior of organisms has included extensive experimentation with animals other than man. Animal research offers many advantages to the experimenter, not the least of which is the fact that the past learning of animal subjects can be made more uniform than that of humans and less likely to introduce confounding variables into an experiment concerned with rather intricate stimulus and response relationships.

RESEARCH AND THEORIES OF LEARNING

Every student who has taken even one course in psychology has heard of Pavlov, the Russian physiologist, who in 1902 began to study conditioned, or learned, reflexes in dogs. Thorndike, an American, published a monograph in 1898 that dealt with the problem-solving behavior of cats. Most present day theories of behavior owe much to the experimental contributions of Pavlov and Thorndike, and to the orientations that developed out of their work. Thorndike, whose early statement of the "Law of Effect" has become the modern principle of reinforcement, was for many years a professor at Teachers College, Columbia University, and his primary interest was educational psychology. Thorndike studied under both William James, philosopher-psychologist and James McKeen Cattell, a pioneer in mental testing, but Thorndike's first laboratory experiments made use of cats, fish, chicks, dogs, and monkeys. Thorndike was one of the first to introduce animals into psychological laboratories and his experimental objective was to study the learning process. In 1911 Thorndike reported his experimental findings in a book entitled *Animal Intelligence*, and two years later he published the first volume of his influential book *Educational Psychology* (1913) in which he presented a theory of learning consisting of several "laws," including the law of effect, the law of exercise, and several others. His law of effect referred to the effect of the consequences of behavior. According to Thorndike, behavior can be thought of as a trial and error process in which the "connections" are strengthened between a stimulus (situation) and a response (behavior) only if success or satisfaction follow the response. Thorndike found that cats, when imprisoned in a box that had a release-operated door, showed a rapid decline over a series of trials in the amount of time required to gain their release from the box and access to food. Interestingly enough, the law of exercise, which was not particularly original with Thorndike, but had been a commonly accepted view in education for centuries, did not survive the experimental tests he gave it. Simple repetition, he concluded, does *not* necessarily strengthen behavior, eliminate errors or increase efficiency, *unless* the law of effect is operable in the situation. In other words, repetition or practice has, by itself, little effect unless the practiced response is reinforced. Thorndike was concerned with all kinds of learning situations, including classroom learning and the educational process. Experimental data of value to him and to others interested in education came from the classroom, from the animal laboratory, and from many practical training and educational situations.

Research in learning followed many different channels during the period between 1900 and 1960. Although Thorndike himself moved almost exclusively to the study of human learning, laboratory animal studies became extremely common in the experimental analysis of learning phenomina. The learned behavior of a white rat, a monkey, or a pigeon is of interest in its own right for many theoretical and practical reasons. However, of primary importance for education has been the development of systematic training procedures and techniques that have been found to be effective in modifying the behavior of experimental subjects in sharply predictable ways. These techniques have been tried out in a number of laboratory and classroom situations using subjects from preschool age through the college level, and the results indicate the operation of the same learning phenomena demonstrated in the animal laboratory. In other words, there are apparently basic psychological learning processes common to many different species of organisms which underlie more obvious biological differences. The law of effect, now called the principle of reinforcement, occupies a central position in almost all current psychological theories of learning. There is little agreement so far concerning the physiological and psychological mechanism of reinforcement, and how and why it operates, but as an empirical principle, reinforcement is widely accepted as an essential element in the learning process.

Many tentatively proposed views of learning make good "common sense," but many common sense notions of learning—like the law of exercise—have not stood the test of laboratory study. Among these untenable notions are those that the threat of punishment (failure, etc.) is necessary as a motivating device; that learning in order to be effective and long-lasting, must be difficult; that correct responses are learned by making mistakes; and that punishment eliminates undesirable behavior. Look closely at these "common sense" statements and note that they are not simply old-fashioned and long-discarded views of learning; some of them continue to be widely accepted and, to some extent, continue to influence existing philosophies of education. In some cases these influences are still present because of conditions that have resulted from the demands of mass education—that is, it may be almost impossible in many classroom situations to provide any kind of motivation *except* threat and anxiety, and punishment may be the *only* immediately effective and available method of terminating undesirable behavior. Ideally, and in the long run, however, these techniques are neither desirable nor particularly effective.

REINFORCEMENT

The analysis of the relationships between events and behavior is complex—far too complex to be considered in any detail here—but there are some points that should be familiar concepts to the teacher. First, *reinforcement* has a specific effect on behavior. Reinforcement has already been defined as the occurrence of a consequence which strengthens the behavior that produced that consequence, that is, the occurrence of an event which increases the probability that the same response will occur again in the presence of the same stimuli. That is, the situational characteristics—the stimuli present when a response is reinforced—become more likely to produce that same response again. When reinforcement occurs, over-all behavior patterns are changed, with the reinforced behavior becoming more likely to recur in that same situation or in response to the same or similar stimuli.

The question "What is a reinforcer?" is not as easily answered as the question "What is its effect?" With laboratory animals, food or water is used to reinforce hungry or thirsty subjects, but with humans the problem is much more complex. Knowledge of correctness of a response has a reinforcing effect, as do many other types of situational and stimulating events. The problem of specifying what will reinforce is made additionally difficult because of the fact that we learn to be reinforced by events that at one time in our lives had no particularly reinforcing effect on us. These secondary or acquired reinforcers may differ tremendously from person to person, although there are undeniably some reinforcers that exert behavioral influences on almost all of us. The "knowledge of results" class of reinforcer—as broad and unspecific as the definition is—is probably the most universal human reinforcer. Recognizing the failure of past efforts to lump all types of reinforcers into one simple class (at one time the most prominent view assigned all reinforcement to physiological drive reduction, or to secondary reinforcers acquired due to their relationship to biological needs) psychologists have recently directed their attention to investigating the many kinds of events that act as reinforcers with emphasis on "how" and "to what extent" (e.g., Harlow, 1958). The physiological considerations need not concern us here; our interest is in the classroom.

You might try to teach a dog to "play dead" or to "fetch" by explaining the behavior pattern to it in the most graphic terms, or by showing the dog what you want it to do, but don't expect to be successful. The verbal command, "Play dead!" means to the dog only the behavior that is reinforced after that command is given. It is as easy—and as difficult—to teach a dog to play dead to any other kind of stimulus: a whistle, a wink, or a nonsense word. The important sequence of events to the dog, or to any other behaving organism, is *stimulus—response—reinforcement.* A child is reinforced for responding "Columbus" to the stimulus "Who discovered America?", but the child learns and remembers the appropriate response for a specific question only when the stimulus-response sequence is immediately followed by some kind of reinforcement. A teacher might say, "How many times must I tell you?" The important question, and the important event, is how many times must the *student tell the teacher,* and be reinforced for responding correctly! Active responding by a teacher is not very important; she already knows the answers, so lectures by the teacher provide practice for the wrong person. The student is the one who is supposed to learn, so it is the student who should be responding actively during the class period.

In an auto-instructional program, reinforcements of various kinds are available to the student. When the student makes a response that he "knows" is right, just the fact that he can go on and complete the response is reinforcing; that is to say, the reinforcement is simply the realization that he knows, or the fact that he is able to proceed to make a response. Contrast this reinforcing event with the case of the student who comes to a test question to which he does not know the answer or who reads a passage in a book that he does not understand; not only is there no response available, but emotional reactions (e.g., frustration) can develop, involving the occurrence of behavior that actively interferes with subsequent learning. Even if the student tries to make responses to material that is not completely clear to him, wrong responses don't fit, and no self-reinforcement is available in the form of "I'm right," or "I understand." The situation is completely different when a program not only makes the correct responses available, but, in addition, indicates to the student that each response is indeed correct, thus providing additional reinforcement. The student then proceeds on to new material and this continuous progress is a kind of moving on to new, novel stimulation, an activity which has also been shown experimentally to be reinforcing.

The programed learning situation includes more than one kind of reinforcement, and includes at least two kinds of student behavior that are being consistently reinforced: each correct response is reinforced, thereby producing the desired relationships between the content of the frames and the responses made to the content; and, in addition, the behavior called paying attention, or attending to stimuli, or reading carefully, is reinforced each time a correct response is made, with the result that the student tends to continue to pay attention and work carefully on each frame. He learns the content of the program, but he is also reinforced for using the program, which results in continued interest and motivation for using the program and responding actively to it.

EXTINCTION

The preceding paragraph dealt with a rather broad look at the student using a program and the general effects of reinforcement. A second concept of importance requires us to look at several other characteristics of the learning process in greater detail. What happens when a response is not reinforced? It is not strengthened, and what is more, it becomes even less likely to occur again in the presence of the same stimuli. When a response occurs and goes unreinforced, the response does not become more firmly "connected" to the stimuli present. The relationship between stimulus and response is actually weakened each time the response goes unreinforced. The weakening of a response is called *extinction,* and the weakening and elimination of unsuccessful behavior as it becomes extinguished is just as important to an organism as the strengthening of successful behavior by the reinforcement it achieves. If a response is not reinforced, by which we mean that the response does not lead to a consequence that is reinforcing, it tends to disappear from an individual's behavioral repertoire, although it may take a very large number of unreinforced occurrences before the response becomes completely extinguished. We do not continue to say hello to a person who never replies; we do not continue to eat in a restaurant where satisfactory food is never served; and we do not continue to read a book that provides no reinforcement for reading—no enjoyment, no understanding, no enlightenment whatsoever. In the case of a dull, confusing, or too difficult textbook, the student may continue to work at it, but generally not for the *positive* reinforcement that should be available as he reads, but rather for the *negative* reinforcement of avoiding failure, a low grade, or a reprimand. Also, by studying, the student may be reinforced only by the fact that he reduces his own aversive emotional responses, guilt due to not studying, or anxiety concerning possible future failure or punishment. In general, psychologists are agreed that negative reinforcement—the avoidance or termination of some aversive condition—is less desirable than positive reinforcement, if for no other reason than the occurrence of undesirable emotional by-products of negative reinforcement situations.

STIMULI AND RESPONSES

Skinner emphasizes the view that a program should be constructed to be almost error free, permitting the student to make only correct responses which can be immediately reinforced. The repetition and occurrence of correct responses permits reinforcement to strengthen the response. If the student responds incorrectly there is no opportunity for the correct response to be reinforced, and what is even more undesirable, the student would be practicing an error in the presence of the stimulus words in the frame.

A theoretical viewpoint slightly different from Skinner's reinforcement emphasis, but which also advocates preventing errors in programs, is Guthrie's learning theory (1952), which suggests that learning the association of stimuli and responses occurs as soon as a response is made, not when reinforcement occurs. According to this view both right and wrong answers are strengthened when they occur, and even correction after an error cannot completely eliminate the tendency for the error to recur later. Guthrie's view, if correct, means that it is essential, not merely desirable, to have programs that are so well constructed that every student makes every response correctly. Responses do not develop in a vacuum, independent of stimulus conditions. A teacher could have a student recite or copy 1492 a number of times, reinforcing the student each time the response occurs, but this procedure is pointless and self-defeating. The response 1492 must be connected to and associated with specific kinds of stimuli. When is the student to emit the response 1492? If the teacher says "When did Columbus first discover the New World?" or "If you have 1500 marbles and lose 8 of them, how many marbles will be left?" or "What Arabic number is represented by the Roman numeral MCDXCII?", the student should respond "1492." A response by itself is meaningless and of no value; a response becomes relevant only when it is appropriately and correctly evoked by stimuli such as questions, environmental events, discussions, books and so on. Reinforcement is apparently essential, not simply to strengthen responses, but to establish consistent and reliable relationships between stimulus contexts and a wide variety of appropriate responses.

A further point here concerns the need for variety in both the form and scope of verbal responses and the stimulus contexts that are to be associated with them. If a teacher requires a student to memorize a definition such as "laissez faire means hands off," without any additional definitions, examples, applications, consequences, advantages and disadvantages in various situations or anything other than the simple form of the definition, it does not matter how well the student memorizes the definition, it is a useless response, without any application whatsoever. Even worse than a simple, one-form-only definition, is the rote memorization of a single, simple example so that the student is forced into the invariable position of being able to define only by saying "laissez faire is when a government doesn't regulate things." Every teacher has heard students answer questions by saying "That is when . . . ," giving a specific example, when the teacher wants, and the goal of instruction should be, an abstraction or a general principle. A student should be able to produce the response "laissez faire" to every example or definition of the principle and should be able to respond correctly to the stimulus "Define laissez faire and give several examples illustrating the principle." The relationships between stimuli and responses make up knowledge and understanding, and it is to the development of these relationships that reinforcement must be applied.

GENERALIZATION AND DISCRIMINATION

In addition to reinforcement and extinction, a third event, *generalization,* occurs to at least some extent with every reinforcement. Generalization is the broadening or far-reaching tendency for a response to occur, not only in the presence of those stimuli actually present during the first occurrence of the response, but in the presence of other, similar stimuli. You may call a friend by name and sometimes make the error of calling a stranger by the same name as your friend, solely on the basis of some characteristic they both have in common, such as red hair, glasses, or almost any other aspect of their over-all appearances. Another way of thinking of generalization is as an inability to tell the difference between stimuli. An animal that has learned to respond to a tone of a particular pitch will respond in similar fashion to a tone of a very different pitch, and a child that has learned the word "doggie" will often call all other four legged animals by the same name, but generalization is actually an extremely complex concept and cannot be defined simply as confusion or lack of discrimination between stimuli. Much of modern education depends on eventual generalization from classroom examples to real life situations. A student learns to solve problems and to respond appropriately to situations presented to him in class, but his classroom successes are of little use to him unless he is able to generalize his learned responses to other situations in which these responses are also appropriate, effective, and successful. The student should be able to handle many situations by recognizing that they resemble, and are in certain critical ways similar to, situations with which he was specifically taught to deal in school.

The opposite of generalization is *discrimination,* the ability to tell the difference between stimuli and to respond appropriately. For example, with reinforced practice you can usually learn to discriminate between identical twins. They might have so many characteristics in common that generalization is originally almost complete, but discrimination can be developed. Just as generalization can be described as responding to similarities, discrimination can be defined as responding to differences.

CONCEPT FORMATION

A fourth point concerns the joint operation of generalization and discrimination in the development of concepts and the formulation of principles and abstractions. *Concept formation* involves generalization within certain specific limits, and the discrimination of those limits. The concept of the physical property "red" generalizes from those specific examples to which the response, red, is originally learned, and eventually applies readily to other new examples that possess the physical property of redness. An individual must be reinforced only for applying the word to objects that *are* red, and he will eventually learn the concept of redness by seeing enough examples of different kinds of red objects which are all called red, but which have only that one characteristic in common. Discrimination enters the picture as he learns to respond with the word red only to red objects, not to blue objects or objects of any other color but red. When he can respond to unfamiliar red objects by saying that they are red, and if he does not mistakenly use the word red in the absence of that color, we say that he has learned the concept, since generalization is complete within the concept, and discrimination is complete between examples of that concept and examples of non-redness. A child also learns to use the word ball as a response to his red ball, and this concept develops as he is reinforced for using the word ball in reference to other balls regardless of their color or size, or any other characteristic that is irrelevant to the concept of ball. Eventually he can identify a ball as such and its color as red, and he is already on the way to learning the concept of color and the concept of shape as characteristics of objects.

Concepts develop as many examples are given and correct responses reinforced so that the one common characteristic of all the examples becomes the effective stimulus for the response that labels the concept, that is, saying "red" as a response to any example of redness if called upon to identify the color. The concept is not sharply defined, until discrimination also develops. This occurs when the learner goes unreinforced for inappropriate responses and learns that red is not a correct response to blue objects. Eventually finer discriminations are made and he learns that pink is not red, and neither is maroon, and he may even learn someday to discriminate between crimson and scarlet.

Successive Approximations

Although the principles of reinforcement, extinction, generalization, discrimination, and concept formation are far more complex than this brief discussion implies, enough has been said to allow us to elaborate on a term that was mentioned only once in passing in Chapter 2. You probably do not remember the term *successive approximations* because you did not actively respond to it, use it, or learn any responses of any kind to it. The method of successive approximations is a technique of training that was originally developed systematically in the animal laboratory, although effective teachers have been using the method for centuries without having a name for it and without even being able to specify all of the systematic steps that it involves. To some extent this technique is simply the programers' approach of "small steps in a logical sequence," but it is more involved than that. Suppose you had to teach a human student some kind of skill without being able to explain to him what he is to do; you can reinforce the desired behavior if it occurs, but you can't tell him what to do so that the behavior will occur in order for you to reinforce it. This is, plainly, the problem that exists when animals are used in the laboratory, yet animals of all kinds have been taught almost unbelievably complex behaviors. You have probably seen trained animal acts, and perhaps you have yourself trained a dog to do tricks and to obey certain commands.

Instruction, training, education, or whatever name it goes by, should *always*, to be maximally efficient, proceed to build upon the existing behavior of the learner, and gradually shape that behavior toward the final goal or terminal objective. Successive approximations means reinforcing, in an ever changing sequence, those behaviors that come progressively and successively closer to approximating the desired performance. This rather complex definition can be clarified by one or two examples. Suppose you want to train a dog, or a laboratory rat or pigeon, to touch a target with its nose. If you wait for the behavior to occur, eagerly waiting to reinforce the response as soon as it occurs, you may wait for such a long time that you will give up in disgust. You might try, ineffectively, to demonstrate by dragging the animal to the target, pushing its nose against the target, and then offering it a food pellet as reinforcement. The method of successive approximations consists of the successful gambit of reinforcing any aspect of the organism's behavior that involves a movement toward the target. If the organism is given reinforcement every time it makes a move toward the target, and only then, the behavior of moving in that direction will quickly increase in frequency. You would then reinforce the animal only for movements that take it closer to the target, until finally the subject arrives there. You would start out by reinforcing behavior that only slightly approximates the response of moving to the target, and would then demand successively closer approximations to the response of touching the target. You would do this by waiting, after the subject arrived in the vicinity of the target, until its head moved a bit toward the target, at which point reinforcement would immediately be provided. The next step consists of requiring continually closer movements until the subject finally contacts the target, and from that point on, reinforcement would be given only when the target is actually touched.

The behavior has now been shaped in the desired direction, and further refinements of the response pattern can be added by following the same careful guidance procedure. Just a little bit of progress at a time, and liberal but systematic reinforcement of the progressive development of the training objective; this is the method. It works, and is based on exactly the same principles and procedures that a good tutor uses, and which underlie auto-instructional programing. Look closely again at this simple account of leading a subject gradually to a desired level of performance, and notice the similarity to the teacher's shaping of the conceptual learning of a student by commenting "That's right, now go on, that's very good so far."

Complex sequences of behavior can be taught by allowing one response to produce the stimulus or signal for the next response. For instance, a laboratory animal can be taught a sequence in which it pulls on a cord which turns on a light, then presses a lever which produces a click, then pushes a wheel that opens the cover of a food tray. The sequence is performed as a chain of responses in the proper sequence, since the wheel opens the food tray only if the bar has been pressed, and the bar produces the click only if the light has been turned on. The sequence then is response (cord pull)—stimulus (light)—response (lever press)—stimulus (click)—response (wheel turn)—stimulus (lid open-food reinforcement) —response (animal consumes reinforcement). This entire chain is taught only one step at a time, and the systematic procedures involved are easily learned by college students in an experimental psychology course in which the training methods are also taught one step at a time (Homme and Klaus, 1957). A motor sequence of this sort, like all stimulus-response sequences, consists of responses to stimuli, each response in turn producing the stimulus for the next response. When unlocking a door you watch the key and the key hole, and when the tip of the key is lined up with the hole (visual stimulus), you push the key into the lock (response). When the key is all the way into the lock (stimulus) you turn the key (response). When the lock clicks (stimulus) you push on the door (response), and when the door is open (stimulus) you enter the house (response). Each response produces a stimulus to which you respond appropriately in sequence. No short cuts are allowed in this example, since it is not appropriate to insert the key into the lock and then walk through the still closed door; the entire sequence must be completed.

Verbal conceptual behavior is of the same sort as motor behavior, since verbal sequences, both in terms of single words and long abstract ideas, involve stimuli and responses. When I say "Verbal conceptual behavior is of the same sort," each word in the sequence is a verbal behavior response and at the same time is a stimulus for the next word in the sentence. Programing of Skinner-type programs is based upon, and incorporates, this same type of relationship between stimuli and responses in human conceptual behavior. Other kinds of programs (see following chapter), notably the Crowder-type programs, are not designed so specifically in terms of a stimulus-response analysis of complex learning, since a large frame, brief question and answer method of program production leaves more of the learning to the student. Skinner relies on the development of specifically arranged-for stimulus and response relationships, while Crowder provides information from which the student must develop his own conceptual chain of stimuli and responses, and do it correctly in order to arrive at the correct answer. Multiple-choice programs tacitly assume that by requiring the student to pay attention and then to arrive at the correct answer according to his own sequencing, the desired, and transferable response sequences will develop.

Perhaps, to the reader, an unnecessary amount of space has been devoted to animal learning, but the experienced teacher can probably recognize in these descriptions the operation of the same principles and the same kind of behavioral development that takes place in the classroom.

Students must be taught to make certain responses to stimuli; responding appropriately to certain stimuli and doing it according to an appropriate sequence is all that knowledge means. Teachers have produced knowledge for thousands of years, without being able to specify the conditions and principles according to which learning develops, and students have learned from unprogramed presentations of materials during that time. What, then, is the promise of programed instruction? Simply that the complexities of modern education and industrial training require the application of all our understanding of instructional techniques so that the limited number of teachers and instructors will be able to provide the most thorough instruction possible for ever-increasing numbers of students. The current development of auto-instructional methods based on specific learning principles is a first and necessary step in the accomplishment of this objective.

4

Variations in Programs

Many proponents of auto-instructional methods agree that a mechanical teaching machine is probably not necessary for the presentation of programed material to the student. Glaser, Homme, and Evans (1959) designed a "programed textbook" which has gained widespread acceptance as a non-mechanical form of presentation of the Skinner-type small frame programs. One type of format for a programed textbook is illustrated in the Appendix. Frame one appears at the top of page 23. The student reads only frame one, ignoring for the moment all other frames on that page. After writing his answer, either directly on the page or in a separate notebook, he turns the page, and finds the correct answer to frame one on page 24, right beside frame two. After comparing his answer with the correct answer, he responds to frame two, turns the page, and so on. He continues on through to the last page, then returns to page one and goes through the same pages again, this time reading the second frame on each page. Since the frames are numbered sequentially, the student is not likely to get lost even due to the unusual nature of the printed pages. This type of page organization prevents the student from seeing previous frames, which might provide helpful prompts at a point where they should no longer be available. Another form of a programed text uses only the right hand pages—the odd-numbered ones—in sequences throughout the book, with the frames on the left hand pages printed upside down, so that when the student gets to the last page he turns the book upside down and works back through it on the even-numbered pages. Other programed booklets have been produced in which frames simply follow each other in order on the same page; this type of presentation is illustrated in Table 1, p. 17.

A machine does have several advantages that a printed booklet of frames does not have. A student using a machine cannot easily cheat by looking at frames out of sequence or by looking at the answers before producing his own responses. Most commercial teaching machines have a "cheat-proof" method of operation which prevents the student from moving inappropriately ahead or backwards in the sequence. However, whether or not cheating is a real problem with students using programed material has not clearly been determined. If the student is required to produce responses that will later be checked by a teacher, he might be motivated to avoid errors by looking ahead in a programed text and copying correct answers, although the real possibility exists that if a program is well written, the student will quickly discover that it requires little more effort to work through the program properly, with a very low error rate, than it does for him to copy the answers without reading the frames. The real payoff comes, of course, with the realization that he has successfully mastered the material while working through the program. When learning is as easy as cheating, and cheating produces no learning, cheating becomes rather pointless. Cheating may not be a problem, but a machine may still have greater inherent interest value for the student, for it might be more fun to operate a mechanical gadget than simply to use a different form of the familiar textbook. Another possibility, of course, is that even if it can be demonstrated that a machine maintains student interest more efficiently than a programed text, the effect of the machine per se will disappear as it becomes a less novel classroom device.

Probably the most influential factor that will determine whether a teaching machine or a programed textbook will become the preferred method of utilizing programed materials is the relative economy of each mode of presentation. Surprisingly enough, economic considerations favor the use of a machine—specifically a film viewing machine. Klaus and Lumsdaine (1960) arrived at this conclusion as a result of an elaborate experiment on the supplementary use of auto-instructional materials in the teaching of high school physics. Approximately 20 per cent of the high school physics course was programed in about 3,000 frames. The program was printed in programed textbook form and was used by some 500 students. The materials prepared for the 500 students required over three and a half tons of paper and 1,440 loose-leaf notebooks. Klaus and Lumsdaine estimate that if they had programed the entire high school physics course each student would have been provided with the equivalent of twenty-two 300-page books containing 16,000 frames, with an estimated cost of $66 per student. The very nature of the programed textbook format restricts the number of frames that can be printed on each page, with a resulting very large total number of pages. A program of 16,000 frames, however, could be reproduced on 400 feet of film for less than $5 per copy. If only two students per year use a roll of film, and one roll lasts for at least five years—a reasonable estimate—the cost per student is only 50 cents. A low cost desk model viewing device might add as little as $1 to the cost per student. A total cost of less than $2 per student, per course, is not unreasonable compared to the cost of the usual high school textbooks.

RESPONSE MODES

One aspect of the use of auto-instructional materials that is flexible and without any single superior method is the mode of responding by the student. Whether material is presented in a film viewer, a teaching machine using sheets or strips of paper, or a programed textbook, the students can be required to write their responses directly in the blanks in the frames, in a separate notebook, or on a strip of paper such as a roll of adding machine tape. There is no particularly good reason why a student should be required to write his response on the program itself, e.g., on the pages of a programed text, thus making it unusable by other students. The simplest and cheapest method of obtaining written responses from students entails the use of a notebook. These can be collected periodically by the teacher, both to check the rate of a student's progress through the program, and to identify topics causing difficulty.

Some (but not all) experimental studies have demonstrated that active responding, whether in the form of writing, speaking, or merely thinking responses, produces significantly more learning than does simply reading the programed material in which no blanks appear and no responses are called for. For this reason, as well as on the basis of the theoretical principles of learning that inspired teaching machines, active responding is generally considered a necessary part of every auto-instructional program. (Conflicting experimental results have been reported on this point. See Chapter 5.) Teachers of motor skills, such as driving a car, skiing, pronouncing words in a foreign language, or writing, have always operated on the premise that overt responding (performance) is absolutely essential if the student's behavior is to undergo the desired modifications. Teachers of motor skills would also agree that a student would be very unlikely to learn any of these activities adequately simply by reading about them, or being told about them. The desired terminal behavior must be practiced and gradually built up in the presence of those cues which eventually are to produce the responses. This is true of motor skills, and advocates of Skinnerian constructed response programs feel that it is also true of abstract conceptual behavior. Several teaching machines that are now commercially available for use with Skinner-type constructed response programs are shown in Figure 3. All of these machines except the Wyckoff Film Tutor require the student to write his response, either directly on the frames themselves, or on a separate roll of paper tape. Each machine has a window that displays first the frame and then the correct response. The Wyckoff Film Tutor incorporates a typewriter keyboard on which the student types out his responses. As he strikes each correct key, the letters appear on the frame projected on the screen before him. As soon as the machine is satisfied that the student is on the way to the correct response, and has performed the necessary components of the response, the machine shows the student the complete correct answer, and then goes on to the next frame. The cost of these machines varies considerably, and dozens of others are available at costs ranging from a few dollars to over one thousand dollars. Basically, all machines serve one purpose: to display a program to a student. The form of a specific program will ultimately determine which machine design is required.

Crowder's Program Design

N. A. Crowder has developed an auto-instructional program design that has several unique features that differentiate it from a Skinner-type program. While Skinner emphasizes the importance of much active, overt responding in the presence of small amounts of specific stimuli, in order to relate stimuli and responses by providing immediate reinforcement, Crowder calls for comparatively few responses for relatively large masses of stimulus material. A Crowder "frame" may be several paragraphs in length, followed by a single multiple-choice question. The student is able to select the correct answer only if he has successfully dealt with the principles described at length in the paragraphs in the frame. The emphasis in this kind of program is not so much on connecting specific stimuli and

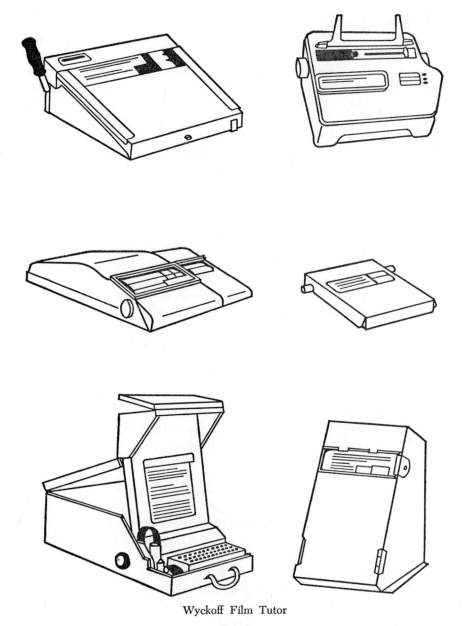

Wyckoff Film Tutor

Fig. 3

Courtesy of American Institute for Research

responses as it is on producing sustained attention to the reading matter. Perhaps the "attention responses" required of the student, or his active manipulation of ideas, which may be necessary before he is able to arrive at the correct answer, can produce learning as effectively as Skinner's small-step frames—a conclusive empirical comparison of these two approaches to learning-from-programs has not yet been performed. Both methods produce learning, so it is reasonable to assume that both will continue to be used until additional research can clarify the question of how programers can best present stimulus material to students. Crowder's multiple-choice questions require the student to recognize the correct answer rather than to produce the answer himself, and selected rather than constructed answers may have a serious drawback in terms of the transfer of learning from this situation to situations in which no choice is offered—to an essay test for example. Educators sometimes question the appropriateness of multiple-choice examinations on the grounds that in "real life" a person is usually required to produce a solution, an answer, or a decision, rather than supply an answer from a short list of specific alternatives, although there are many cases in which an individual faces only a limited number of choices in his decision-making. Many of the available Crowder programs side step this type of objection effectively by requiring active problem solving behavior by the student before any of the listed alternatives appears plausible as an answer. If a Skinnerian frame and a Crowder-type frame both produce the same type of covert (thinking) responses in a correct usage sequence of ideas and relationships, there is no reason to prefer one over the other. When a student arrives at the correct answer in the presence of the relevant stimuli and is immediately reinforced for his answer, the key event that is strengthened is the sequence of thought responses that occurred—including the correct answer. In a Skinnerian frame the student writes his answer, but before he can do so he must arrive at that answer and decide what it is. The writing is an anti-climax which is required of him only to guarantee that the covert behavior takes place and that he does not skim the material without dealing actively with it. The "active responding" necessary for learning is not the writing or the button pushing or the page turning or any other motor response required by a program, but consists of the covert verbal behavior that the student goes through when he becomes actively and intellectually involved with the concepts that he reads. As long as the program correctly produces this behavior on the part of the student, by requiring him to do it before he can write an answer down or identify the correct button on a multiple-choice machine, it is probably irrelevant how he is made to demonstrate his knowledge.

CORRECTIVE BRANCHING

Probably the most unique feature of Crowder's programs is the variability which is built into them. Crowder has described this feature as "intrinsic programing," in which the student takes a route through the program that is determined by his own response to each question. By contrast, a Skinner program is "extrinsically programed," that is, the route or sequence of frames is more rigidly established by the programer and less by the student. The alternate routes Crowder uses in his programs are called "branches" and are employed as a method of foreseeing and diagnosing possible and probable sources of misunderstanding by the student. While Skinner feels that errors should be prevented—since the ultimate objective is correct responses—Crowder capitalizes on each mistake by providing corrective feedback, explaining a little more about the concept on which the question is based, along with information about why the specific answer is not correct.

Branching as a method of routing the student through a program is not restricted to Crowder's programs, but his method of incorporating branches is different from those sometimes used in the Skinner-type programs. A Crowder-type program is constructed in such a way that every student comes into contact with a specific set of frames and, in addition, students who make errors are routed to other frames which are never seen by students who make no errors, or who make different kinds of errors. In a Skinner-type program all students generally complete every frame, but students may sometimes be returned to earlier frames following errors in order to repeat certain parts of the program before being permitted to continue on to later frames. Ideally, of course, every program should permit the student to proceed without making any errors; however, to the extent that a program is not perfect for all students, some branching or re-cycling technique might be provided. Regardless of the care with which a program is written, tested, and revised, an occasional student will misinterpret a frame or make a spurious error which will sometimes completely disrupt the sequence and interfere with his progress. The more capable students do not usually need as much repetition or as many examples as less rapid learners, and to avoid boring these faster learners a program can include check points, consisting of three or four demanding questions. A student who makes any errors on these questions is told to continue on through the detailed sequence. If a student gets all of the test items correct, he may be told to skip ahead to a later point in the program, bypassing repetition that he does not need, but which is available for students who do need it. Also the program may include some form of corrective routing, or the student may be instructed to consult the teacher whenever difficulties appear.

Crowder has developed a special booklet design which differs from the programed textbook by having each page contain only a single stimulus unit, followed by a multiple-choice question. The pages of the book are numbered sequentially, but the material is assigned to pages randomly and the student is directed to turn to a page number which is determined by his choice of an answer to each question. For example, on page one he may read several short paragraphs and then a multiple choice question that has a different page number printed beside each of the answer choices:

If your answer is:	Turn to page:
Choice a	5
Choice b	23
Choice c	10
Choice d	19

Suppose that the correct answer is Choice b, and that the student turns to page 23. He is told that his choice is the correct answer, and is then told to continue reading the rest of page 23 and to answer the next multiple-choice question at the bottom of that page. Each of the incorrect alternatives on page 1 sends the student to a different page where he is informed that his choice is not correct, told why it is not correct, and provided with more information designed to help him answer the question correctly. Then the student is told to return to page 1 and to select the correct answer. The correct sequence is from page 1 to page 23, with three alternate routes to handle students who don't select the correct answer (Figure 4). Page 23 contains another multiple-choice question which has only one correct answer and three incorrect answers, each of which leads to its respective correcting branch. An errorless route through the first seven frames might follow this sequence: 1—23—7—25—12—3—18. It is assumed that the student who follows this sequence has adequately learned the material on each page in the series, and it is further assumed that the alternate response-determined branches have adequately corrected any misconceptions or misunderstanding on the part of the students who have made errors, but who have eventually also reached page 18. The seven-item sequence, including alternate branches, might

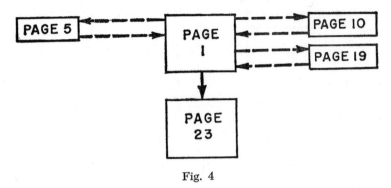

Fig. 4

be diagrammed as shown in Figure 5. Notice that an error on page 12 is considered relatively serious, and that one of the correcting branches from that page requires that the student complete more than a page of related questions before returning to page 12 for another try at the correct answer. A total of 25 pages is necessary for the seven basic steps and the related branches in this example, and a student may come into contact with any number of these pages, from an errorless seven to a maximum of 25 if he chooses every possible wrong answer. The student, by his responses, determines not only his route through the program, but the number of steps through which he proceeds.

Crowder's booklet, called commercially a TutorText, and descriptively a "scrambled textbook," has a machine counterpart in which the pages are printed on 35mm film and are projected onto a viewing screen (Figure 6). Beside the screen is a panel of buttons on which the student punches the number corresponding to his choice, and the machine, which can store up to 10,000 images, quickly produces the selected page image.

The use of multiple-choice answers has the drawback that a student can simply select answers randomly, not really caring whether he is right or wrong, but, like the problem of cheating, this difficulty may not appear if the student discovers that it is not very much more difficult to "play the game" than it is to select answers without first trying to arrive at the correct answer himself. If a student does actively engage in the appropriate problem solving behavior and arrives at the correct answer, then there is probably little significance attached to the form of his overt response; that is, if he considers the problem and arrives by himself at the correct answer, it probably doesn't matter whether he then writes it down, identifies it in a list, pushes a button, or says it out loud. From the point

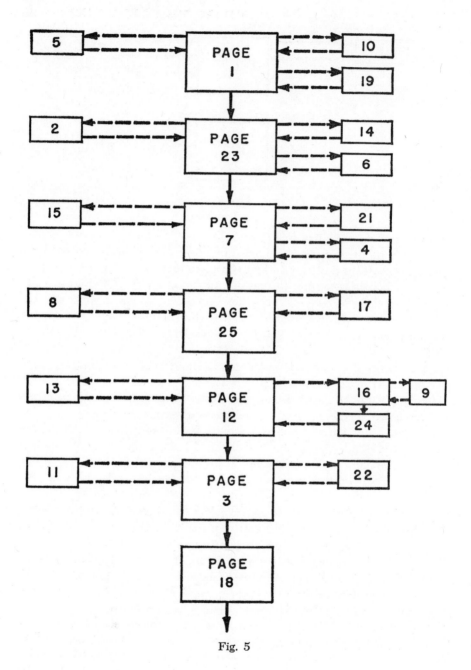

Fig. 5

Fig. 6

Courtesy of American Institute for Research

of view of the learner, as was pointed out before, each of these activities is secondary to the critical event of arriving at the correct answer.

MULTIPLE-CHOICE RESPONSES

Skinner and Crowder have produced programs that differ in two striking physical characteristics:

	Size of unit	*Type of response*
Skinner	Small frames	Constructed
Crowder	Large units	Selected (multiple-choice)

A third type of program, similar in appearance to Pressey's early programs, makes use of small frames with a multiple-choice mode of responding. There are also existing examples of the other possible combination—large frames and constructed responses. Initially, in most non-branching multiple-choice programs, the learning occurs according to a form of guided trial and error, in which the feedback provides reinforcement or correction, whichever is appropriate, with the emphasis on reinforced practice later on in the program. Another possible use of multiple-choice programs is in conjunction with a standard textbook or other presentation, so that the program provides additional strengthening of the acquired ideas and also acts as a self-test method of identifying trouble areas for the student. The producers of programs that use multiple-choice answers emphasize the point of view that the student is learning not only to arrive at and then select the correct answer, but to discriminate accurately between correct and incorrect conclusions or statements. Of course, if the student is able *only* to discriminate correct from incorrect statements, but cannot produce the correct one himself, he is in much the same position as the student who says, "I can't think of his name, but I'm sure I'd recognize it if I heard it." Ability to discriminate between stimuli is not always enough; in many situations the student must be able to produce complete and complex responses himself, and it remains the responsibility of the program to see that this becomes possible. Skinner has objected to multiple-choice questions on two grounds; that a good program should avoid errors by the student, and that it is probably not a good idea to let students read untrue statements (the wrong choices), for someday the student might make an incorrect statement, and then defend it on the grounds that he knows that he read it somewhere.

The differences between the programs described in these chapters, and the side issue of the machine versus a special book containing a program, are only a few of the differences that have developed in this rapidly growing field. As was mentioned before, the basic features that are common to all auto-instructional methods, the identifying characteristics that distinguish auto-instruction from simple audio-visual aids, is the self-paced active response by the student, followed by immediate feedback (reinforcement) from the program. Published programs of many types are now available, and programing is being conducted at every educational level from pre-school through elementary and secondary grades, to college level courses. Fortunately, basic research of many necessary varieties is being conducted to clarify the issues and to determine which are the most fruitful of the techniques already available to would-be programers.

Undoubtedly, techniques will eventually be developed by which systematic covert active responding can be produced without requiring students to construct all of their responses, nor to select from listed alternatives. Techniques which can guarantee that correct responding will occur in the thinking that the student performs will eliminate the need for the student to perform overt responses. *Active* responding is essential, but it need not all be overt. If a correct response (thinking) follows an appropriate stimulus, learning occurs. Undoubtedly, criterion frames which call for the complex responses that have been built up will always be a part of auto-instruction, serving as both intermittent knowledge of results (on more simple frames the student will know he is correct without being told so) and as an achievement indication to the teacher. Programs of the future will also include combinations of several different response modes, a range of frame sizes, and a wide variety of other characteristics. The terminal objectives of most courses will require a variety of techniques,

techniques that will be developed by means of the same type of careful experimentation that has produced existing auto-instructional methods. The experimentation and the questions of current interest, which are described in the following chapter, are necessary steps in the developmental sequence leading to the goal of developing the best possible educational methodologies.

5

Experimental Results

College students who had used an early version of a psychology program which has since been revised and published in programed textbook form (Holland and Skinner, 1961) were asked to give their reactions to the program in order to assist their instructors in deciding whether or not to use the program again the following semester. Some of the representative comments were:

"I learned concepts clearly from the program that I had trouble understanding when reading and studying the book."

"The program makes the course less challenging since the basic principles are presented on a silver platter. It seems as though individual initiative is destroyed; there is no need to struggle with the concepts because they are drilled into the student."

"I think the program helped a lot in the long run, but the frames go so slowly that while doing them I'm not sure I'm accomplishing very much."

"I feel that I learned more from the program than from either of the assigned texts."

"After working for an hour or two I felt that I had accomplished something, but the fact that I could learn so much so fast made long reading assignments harder to do."

"Sometimes the repetition got boring, but the fact that the frames were

51

not always worded in the same way made the repetition help me to remember."

"I liked the repetition, as it gave me a clearer understanding of the concepts."

The general tone of the comments was overwhelmingly favorable, although almost half of this group (11 of 24 students) had at least one criticism to offer. These brief comments were selected because they cover broadly the range of views that were expressed. Obviously, subjective conclusions by the students concerning the relative amounts of learning from program and textbook are not necessarily correct, but they are significant indications of students' attitudes toward the use of programs. The characteristic to which students most frequently objected was the small-step sequencing of frames, while at the same time the characteristic most appreciated was the thoroughness with which principles were understood upon completion of the program. These two characteristics are closely related or perhaps one is cause and the other effect. These students liked the *consequences* of small steps and varied repetition, but tended to dislike too repetitive sequencing of the conceptual development itself. The only student who said that he would prefer not to use programs in other courses was the author of the comment concerning "silver-platter" learning. He was an A student who indicated that, for him, part of the fun of learning was the successful hard work that it entailed. Other reactions to the same program have been reported by Holland (1959). Approximately 180 of his students were asked to complete a questionnaire with the results shown in Table 2.

The last alternative to item 4 was selected by almost one-third of the students, perhaps indicating that the students tended to move too quickly through the frames, apparently feeling that they were not permitted to stop until a major unit had been completed. One implication here is that the teacher's role is important in "following up" the program by insuring that each student actively discusses the material and its implications.

The ease of learning through the use of a program and the slow progression through a series of small steps often alarm many students because of the absence of difficulty. A student knows immediately whether a response is right or wrong, but some students express discomforture at not really knowing how thoroughly they understand the broader aspects of the subject matter. Since at no point in the program is a student severely pressed or presented with an obstacle, he does not experience the type of reinforcement that comes with struggling with obviously difficult material and successfully and consciously mastering it. Perhaps frequent tests should be made available to the student for the purpose of self-evaluation

TABLE 2

(from Holland)

1. If machines had not been used this year I believe:

84.3%   I would have gotten less out of the course
12.1%   it would have made no difference
 3.4%   I would have gotten more out of the course

2. In comparing work on the machine with studying the text, I felt that, *with the same amount of time and effort:*

45.3%   I learned much more on the machine
33.0%   I learned somewhat more on the machine
 0.9%   there was no difference
16.9%   I learned somewhat more from the text
 3.8%   I learned much more from the text

3. If I were to take another introductory course in a science or similar field I would:

76.6%   prefer to have machines used for part of the course
13.5%   prefer not to have machines used
 9.9%   not care whether machines were used or not

4. At some time during the course I felt that, in being taught by machines,

22.3%   I was being treated like an experimental organism
 2.7%   the use of machines reflected upon my dignity as a human being
62.5%   the instructor was trying to teach me as much as possible with a given expenditure of my time and effort
30.4%   I was missing many opportunities to reflect on material and consider its implications

(Responses to item 4 total more than 100% because some students marked more than one answer.)

of progress. It would not be particularly surprising if frequent tests turned out to be an essential part of the feedback needed and welcomed by the student. There is no reason why such tests could not be built into a program as check points at which a student evaluates his own progress, and at which the teacher determines whether the student needs remedial program contact, remedial teacher contact, or is ready to go on to the next part of the course—either in the form of teacher-student interaction or further progress through the program.

The repetition that is characteristic of small steps often appears unnecessary to the student using the program, and even slow learners and students with poor retention who need repeated practice may tend to question the necessity for frequent repetition of the same concept. This difficulty cannot be ignored since it can affect the students' interest and attention to the program and because students discriminate the fact that various forms of the same response typically are required in succession over a series of frames as a concept is developed. Students who have made this discrimination about the structure of a program often tend to respond on the basis of this expectation by repeating the same response automatically from one frame to another, even though such set repetition is usually guarded against by the programers. Ideally, repetition of a concept should be varied within the bounds of that concept, so that each frame dealing with the same principle does not simply provide practice, but adds more knowledge and generality to the concept. This kind of repetition is not only more psychologically sound, but also tends to eliminate negative reactions by students who might otherwise perceive some of the frame sequences as rather dull, rote drill. Although you might expect that students will always tend to object to small steps, and might also object to having to write a response to every frame, Klaus and Deterline (1961) found that high school students who evaluated a 1600 frame program in atomic physics did not feel that the program generally either moved too slowly or too rapidly, even though the program consisted of small steps with extensive, varied repetition. These students did not object to writing a response to every frame. They indicated that they usually knew that each response was correct even before looking at the answers, but they felt that the correct answers were necessary so that they could check their responses and have any errors corrected immediately. In commenting randomly on the program, almost one-third of the students expressed the view that having to write responses was valuable, since it forced them to remain alert and helped them learn.

Feldhusen (1961) has reported reactions of college students to autoinstructional programs and teaching machines. In response to the question "How effective would a teaching machine be in promoting learning of new concepts and skills in comparison with a textbook covering the same material?", approximately 92 per cent of the students felt that the teaching machine could be more effective, while approximately 4 per cent favored the textbooks. The remaining students favored neither method over the other. An interesting finding in this study was the popularity of the classroom lecture and the relative unpopularity of textbooks. Students were asked, "Which do you think you would prefer to do to learn some new material?" The student responses are shown in Table 3. Categories a, d, f, and g all involve use of teaching machines and approximately 92 per cent of the students chose one of these four categories. Similarly, categories c, e, f, and g involved a classroom lecture and the preference here was also approximately 92 per cent. A textbook used with a machine attracted only about 6 per cent, and a textbook used with a lecture was favored by only about 5 per cent, while the lecture-teaching machine combination was

TABLE 3

(from Feldhusen, 1961)

Percentage of 129 college students choosing each method of presentation

a.	Study on a teaching machine	1.6%
b.	Read a textbook	0.0%
c.	Listen to a lecture	2.3%
d.	Machine plus textbook	6.2%
e.	Lecture plus textbook	5.4%
f.	Machine plus lecture	23.3%
g.	Machine plus textbook plus lecture	61.2%

chosen by 23 per cent. The only two-mode combination that attracted many students was the combination of lectures and teaching machines. The textbook was a significant selection only when offered in conjunction with both of the other two teaching methods. In general, these students felt that the individual pacing of auto-instruction was its primary advantage, while the primary disadvantages indicated were a reduction of contact between teacher and student, and a mechanical, unintellectual kind of learning.

Klaus and Deterline (1961) found that students given a choice of teachers, textbooks, and programs, tended to prefer teachers and programs. No students in their sample indicated a preference for teachers, programs, or textbooks alone. No students preferred teachers plus textbooks without programs if programs were also available. All the students wanted both a teacher and a program, and approximately 50 per cent indicated that if they had both a teacher and a program, they would like an additional textbook. These students did not want programs to replace teachers, but did prefer programs to unprogramed textbooks.

The reports of student reactions in this chapter must be interpreted cautiously, since all the student attitudes reported here were based on very limited student experience. The students who made these comments had used only one program for a relatively short period of time compared to the many years of experience that they had had with teachers, textbooks, and the traditional classroom. The programs were a novelty and the students were actually very unskilled and inexperienced evaluators. Another point that must be remembered, particularly by teachers who question students informally in order to obtain some reactions to the classroom use of programs, is the effect that the teacher's bias can have on the stated views of the students. An enthusiastic disciple of programed instruction who carefully describes auto-instructional methods to her students is almost certain to receive favorable comments when she asks for the students' views. A skeptical presentation on the other hand, or the use of a poor program to illustrate the method, will just as surely produce unfavorable comments. The statements made by students should be freely given without inappropriate biasing by a well-meaning instructor. The comments made by students, whether identifying characteristics of programs that bother them or please them, or simply expressing satisfaction or dissatisfaction with auto-instruction, provide useful information to programers who can take these reactions into consideration in subsequent programing. Of less value are comments concerning guesses or estimates of the effectiveness of auto-instruction, or about the possible consequences of the use of programs, since only empirical research findings can answer questions of that nature.

EXPERIMENTAL DATA

Students' verbal reactions to auto-instruction are as varied as their responses to textbooks and teachers, and although their reactions to programs tend to be favorable, little reliance or confidence in the effectiveness of auto-instruction can be based solely on evaluations of this sort. The critical question concerning auto-instruction is how well does it accomplish all its objectives, and to what extent does it produce all the advantages attributed to it? Unfortunately, this is a complicated question which cannot be completely answered on the basis of the data now available. Most, but not all, of the more elaborate experiments that have so far been performed have shown varying degrees of superiority of programed over unprogramed materials, and the returns are still coming in.

Most experiments in this area might be assigned to one of two general categories: (a) field-study experiments that involve the use of programed materials in actual classroom situations, using existing classes of students who are engaged in taking the course for which the programs were written, or (b) laboratory studies in which relatively small groups of experimental subjects are given programed materials outside of any classroom courses or situations. In experiments of the latter sort, two different versions of a program might be written, each version given to a different group of subjects, and their relative achievement scores compared. There are many complicated problems involved in any type of educational research, and research with auto-instructional material is no exception. For some purposes large numbers of experimental students are needed, and in certain cases it is essential that many individual subjects, and even many groups of subjects, be carefully matched on the basis of intelligence, age, past achievement, or any of a host of other pertinent characteristics. The experimental evaluation of auto-instruction has produced several areas of active controversy, and many years will pass before most of the critical questions are answered to the satisfaction of all concerned. Some of the controversial topics will be mentioned briefly in passing, but for our purposes most of the minor research questions can safely be ignored. The following experimental findings are by no means a comprehensive compilation of all the studies that have been reported, but they do indicate the types of problems being studied, the experimental procedures which have been used, and the kinds of results that have been obtained.

Pressey (1950) has reported a series of studies in which students used a specially devised punchboard to answer multiple-choice questions. Corresponding to each test question was a row of four holes in the top of the board. The student was instructed to insert the point of his pencil into the hole corresponding to his answer for each test question. If the student put the pencil point into the correct hole the pencil punctured an answer sheet sandwiched between the top and bottom layers of the punchboard. If the student inserted the pencil point into any of the other three holes for that question, the point made a mark on the answer sheet but could not fully penetrate it because of the unpunched answer key under each of the incorrect choices. Each question was constructed in the same way; under the punchboard hole corresponding to the correct answer, the answer key had a hole in it, hidden by the answer sheet. The student discovered the hole in the answer key for a particular question when he had selected the correct answer to that question, and when he made an error he discovered that immediately also. The characteristics of auto-instruction present in this device are obvious: immediate correction or reinforcement, individual pace setting, and active responding. Having used three kinds of subject matter material—rote, meaningful but unorganized, organized and meaningful—Pressey reported that students did learn new material successfully from the punchboard multiple-choice programs, demonstrating significant reductions in number of errors when the same punchboard multiple-choice test was taken the second time. Under ordinary test conditions, of course, students would not score much higher on a multiple-choice test if they immediately took it a second time without having any opportunity for additional learning. In classroom usage too, Pressey found that subject matter on which the students were given practice using the punchboards was learned faster and retained longer than parts of the subject matter which had to be learned from reading.

Ferster and Sapon (1958), in one of the first reported experiments that developed out of Skinner's research projects, demonstrated that an auto-instructional program in introductory German could, without aid of a teacher, successfully teach students the equivalent of a one semester beginning German course and could do it in about half the number of hours ordinarily spent by students in the classroom and in doing homework. The subjects used by Ferster and Sapon were volunteers and all subjects used the same program. The only comparison made was the total number of hours spent by the experimental subjects as compared to the usual course time. This experiment was more a "feasibility" study than an analytical study designed to compare various teaching methods. The program was of the constructed response variety and included the characteristics of active responding, immediate feedback, and so on. There have been other studies designed to test the feasibility of auto-instruction in various types of courses, and the results tend to be in the same direction—if it can be learned it can be programed, and auto-instruction has either time or efficiency advantages, or both. In a military situation, for example, three experiments were performed comparing Crowder-type scrambled books with standard classroom teaching methods. Students using only the scrambled books learned about as much as the students who received normal classroom instruction, and they were able to do so in about half the amount of time. (Hosmer and Nolan, 1960).

Coulson and Silberman (1960), and Fry (1960) found that multiple-choice responding took significantly less time than constructed-answer responding. However, these two studies also indicated that although multiple-choice response programs typically take less time than constructed-response programs, the amount of learning that can be demonstrated by an examination given upon completion of the programs depends in part upon the type of examination given. If the examination is composed of essay or completion questions, a constructed-response program apparently prepares the students more efficiently for the examination. Both constructed-response programs and selected-response programs seemingly do equally well in preparing students for multiple-choice tests.

At this point a hoary educational question appears: which is a better indication of learning, an essay test or a multiple-choice test? Introductory educational psychology texts point out that students develop different study techniques for preparing for each of these types of examinations. The point is also made that students who prepare for an essay examination can demonstrate their knowledge on a multiple-choice test as well, while students who prepare for a multiple-choice test typically do not do as well if given an essay examination. The experimental results mentioned in the preceding paragraph tend to support that view, since students using a constructed-response program are, in effect, preparing for a completion or short essay exam and they perform equally well on either an essay or multiple-choice test. On the other hand, the students using a multiple-choice program can be thought of as preparing for a multiple-choice test, and although they do as well on the multiple-choice test as the students who used the constructed-response program, they are inferior in their performance on essay or completion tests. Constructed-response programs are designed specifically to teach students to produce —not select—correct answers, while multiple-choice programs tend more often to teach students to discriminate right from wrong answers under conditions in which both the right and the wrong answers are available to the student, and from which he is to make his choice. Obviously the question of constructed versus selected responses—both in programing and in testing—is important enough to merit additional experimentation in this area.

Coulson and Silberman (1960) also studied the relative efficiency of programs that were composed of different numbers of frames. Starting with a complete set of 104 frames, 48 repetitious frames were discarded, leaving a shorter program of 56 frames that covered the same material. The longer program was considered to consist of small steps between frames while the shorter program was described as consisting of larger steps. Step size refers to the rate at which frames progress through the coverage of a particular concept. Twelve frames covering a particular point are said to proceed through the material in smaller steps than four frames covering the same point. Coulson and Silberman found that the longer, smaller step program produced significantly higher scores on the criterion examination. Evans, Glaser, and Homme, in an earlier study (1959) had obtained similar results showing the superiority of smaller steps. They took a 51 frame program, eliminated repetitious frames to produce a 30 frame and a 40 frame program, and then added 17 additional frames to produce a 68 frame program. Each of the four programs, 30, 40, 51, and 68 frames respectively, was then used by a different group of students. The results indicated that fewer errors were produced by the smaller step (more frames) programs, both in the actual responses made to the frames and in an immediate as well as a retention examination. The most efficient program, however, was the 51 frame program, not the 68 frame program, suggesting that there is probably a maximal number of frames beyond which further repetition has no appreciable effect.

In the same report, Evans, et al., reported finding that programed material produced greater learning, but required more time than standard textbook coverage of the same material. They also found, unexpectedly, that students who used programed material but did not actually write down their responses did better than students who wrote their responses to each frame. Results in the same direction have been reported by Goldbeck & Briggs (1960) and by Roe (1960), both of whom found that carefully sequenced small steps produced the same amount of learning whether students simply read them or were required to make overt written responses. The programs used in these three studies were all very short, less than 100 frames.

Results in the opposite direction were obtained by Holland (1960), who found that students who wrote down their responses did better than students who merely "thought" their responses and also did better than students who read versions of the frames in which no words were left blank. Holland later repeated his experiment (1961) and obtained results supporting his original findings. Holland's finding, that students who had to construct answers learned more than students who simply read the complete frames with all the blanks filled in, is more in line with the theoretical expectations than are the results reported by Golbeck and Briggs and by Roe. Most programers would expect that active, overt responding has significant advantages over "passive" reading. Holland's data indicate that even with careful, small step sequencing, a program is not completely adequate unless it guarantees that the student will respond actively to each small step. Nevertheless, there apparently are conditions under which this is true and conditions under which this is not the case. Perhaps the length of the program is the critical determining factor, since Holland made use of a long program, while the studies that showed no advantage in overt responding all made use of very short programs; or perhaps the capabilities of the subjects in respect to the level of the program is the significant variable. Only detailed experimentation will answer this question.

Holland also analyzed the final criterion examination in terms of the degree to which each test question was relevant to the program. Since the program did not specifically and completely cover every point that was mentioned in the regular textbook, an examination item might refer to a concept that the program had not discussed at all. This kind of examination item was called "irrelevant" in regard to the program. An examination question whose content was thoroughly and completely covered by the program was "highly relevant" to the program, and examination questions that could be partly answered on the basis of program coverage were considered to be "partially relevant" to the program. A question to which the program was irrelevant could be answered on the basis of knowledge acquired only from sources other than the program, e.g., the textbook. Holland found that, in general, more students answered the highly relevant items correctly than answered the "program irrelevant" items correctly. The 152 students correctly answered, on the average, 70 per cent of the highly relevant items, 50 per cent of the partially relevant items, and 40 per cent of the irrelevant items. That is, the "irrelevant" items dealt with ideas that had not been covered by the program so these ideas may be assumed to have been learned either from the textbook, the lectures, or some other source, but *not* from the program. The highly relevant items could have been learned from the program, textbook, lecture, or other combinations of sources. The teacher might look at this experiment as indicating that in this one specific case the program produced an increase in test scores from about 40 per cent correct to 70 per cent correct, an impressive increase, but one that could be at least partly the result of the additional time that the students spent on the topics covered by the program, that is, the program provided additional student contact with some concepts but not with others. Even if the programed presentation was no more effective than the textbook, the additional contact might be expected to add some improvement to the students' test scores.

The first really extensive field study designed to test the effectiveness of auto-instruction was conducted by Klaus and Lumsdaine (1960, 1961). A Skinner-type program consisting of some 3,000 frames was constructed in programed textbook form to cover approximately six weeks of the standard high school physics course. Specifically, it covered the topics of static electricity and direct current, and the reflection and refraction of light. Classes from fifteen Pittsburgh high schools provided a total of approximately 450 subjects. Apart from the programs all students were given classroom lectures, laboratory demonstrations, the televised Harvey E. White physics films, and a textbook. The students also performed laboratory demonstrations themselves in supervised lab periods. The standard teaching procedure, it is clear, subjected the students to a rather broad barrage of physics presentations. The experimental design was rather complex: some classes used all sections of the program, some classes used only one or two of the sections, and some did not use any part of the program. For each section of the physics course then, all students used a standard textbook and attended classroom lectures, laboratory sessions, and televised lectures. In addition, students in some of the high schools used the program for additional coverage of the same topics. Unless the standard teaching procedures were producing the maximum potential learning by all students, any increase in learning on the part of the students using the program could simply be attributed to the added *time* spent on the program. To add a means of measuring any possible effects of sheer additional study time, some classes were given individual workbooks paralleling the coverage of the program. Under these conditions the performance of the students using the workbooks could be compared with that of students whose additional time was spent working on the programs.

The results indicated that the classes using the programs did better on an achievement test than students who had used neither program nor workbook. The workbook classes were superior to the classes having neither workbook nor program, but were inferior in performance to the classes who had used the programs. These results are impressive for several reasons. The two most striking ones are related to the classroom conditions under which the experiment was performed. The students were already being taught physics by several integrated methods, yet, even beyond all this coverage, the programs were still able to produce significant gains in performance levels. Program usage was voluntary, yet a sizable percentage of the students that had been given the programs did work through most of the frames. Even though the scores of those students who had completed only small portions of the program were included in the statistical analysis, the test score differences were significant.

In a second study five classes in each of two other high schools were used experimentally in a slightly different fashion. In some classes the students used the programs instead of having a teacher, and in the other classes the students had a teacher as well as the programs. Comparison of the teacher plus program versus the program alone indicated that no significant differences in achievement were produced by either approach. In other words this second study indicated that the teacher did not add to the level of achievement produced by the program alone, so that a teacher's time, instead of being used to teach the type of material contained in the programs, could be saved for more important instructional functions.

These examples represent only a few of the experiments that have been performed using programed materials, and they were selected because they represent the kinds of variables that have been investigated. The findings are important because the future development of programs and their application in education and industrial training will be greatly influenced by the rapidly growing store of experimental data. In writing programs of the small frame, constructed-response variety for example, programers have profited from Holland's (1960) findings which indicate that writing a frame is not simply a matter of writing a sentence or two and then striking out one or two words, leaving them for the student to fill in. The response called for should be the response to be learned and an irrelevant word or phrase produces significantly less learning. If a frame is written with irrelevant blanks the student must still read the frame in order to produce the response, and certainly any written response at all is "overt responding," but if a student completes the blanks in a sentence by filling in the words that have relatively little importance, the full potentialities of the program cannot be realized. A frame might read, "The Greek letter sigma (Σ) means add, or sum the numbers. Σ, for example, means add up all the numbers represented by the symbol X." If the words "all" or "symbol" are left blank the student learns very little by filling them in. The key words, "add," and "add the numbers" are the words that the student should be able to produce in the presence of the stimulus, and these, therefore, are the words that the student should be required to use as overt responses. Klaus (1960) has suggested that *before* a frame is written, the key response or responses to be called for should be determined and then the frame should be written toward that end.

As we saw in earlier chapters, programing is a still developing art, continuously influenced by the feedback that programers get from student responses and from the results of experimental studies like those described above.

EVALUATION

What are we to conclude from the experiments that have specifically tested auto-instructional programs under various conditions of use, and in varied form? From the point of view of the psychologist whose specialty is learning theory, no final conclusions are as yet warranted, nor are they necessary. Too few studies, generally with many experimental conditions confounded or uncontrolled, have been performed to indicate very much about the relative merits of constructed responses versus selected responses, branching versus no branching, small steps versus large steps, or short frames versus long frames, or to answer questions concerning the role of a mechanical "teaching machine," reinforcing and confirming methods, difficulty levels, etc. The experiments that have been performed so far have generally answered relatively simple and specific questions for the experimenter or have been designed to convince other people that programed, auto-instructional methods "work" and have great promise for training and education. The psychologists who first responded to Skinner's lead were either experimental psychologists whose primary activity was human and animal experimentation that dealt with the complex principles and theories of learning, or experimental psychologists who were actively engaged in the development of training methods and devices (e.g., industrial and military), plus some psychologists and educators who were interested in the general area of education and educational media. There is a vast body of experimental literature—to which these same experimenters have contributed—that gives considerable confidence to the psychologist whose specialty is learning theory, because the empirical basis for the auto-instructional approach to learning is solid enough that the general principles are hardly questioned. The enthusiasm that has led many experimental psychologists to transfer from the study of basic learning phenomena—using memory drums, concept formation stimuli, mazes, lever-pressing devices, and discrimination equipment—to the development and testing of auto-instruction, is at least partly due to the fact that auto-instruction is not a radical development of a particularly novel idea; it is a not-very-extreme extrapolation from principles already well defined and a direct application of reliable methods of producing learning in experimental subjects.

Many experimental psychologists who are presently conducting large scale studies of the effectiveness of auto-instruction are, of course, trying to answer their own questions about program characteristics. More importantly, however, they are also attempting to demonstrate objectively, empirically, and systematically, just how effective the methods of programed learning can be. Data must be available and every advance in the technology of programing must be empirically evaluated and validated if acceptance and wide spread use of programs—with or without teaching machines—is to come about. This is not to say that infatuation with auto-instruction has replaced scientific objectivity; the limitations and necessary modifications of the present views on programing and program usage are as keenly sought by the programers as are examples in which present views of potentialities are supported. The experimental literature dealing with programs in use by students is growing steadily, and many large scale studies that will be of several years duration are currently in progress.

In addition to the specific questions of programing techniques, program designs, and problems of the sort described in this chapter, experiments have been performed in the teaching of remedial reading, remedial English, and remedial mathematics. They have been especially devised for the mentally retarded and for the exceptionally bright. Nursery school children have successfully learned certain elementary number concepts, first graders have learned about molecular theory, and some college and high school students have already encountered experimental programs in several foreign languages, many branches of mathematics, most of the natural sciences, logic, statistics, and music. The list grows steadily longer. Both Encyclopedia Britannica Films, and Grolier, publishers of Encyclopedia Americana, have large-scale programing projects under way, and there are many other commercial producers of programs in what promises to be a highly competitive field of endeavor. Many industrial and military training organizations have already added programed materials to their training courses, and extensive research projects have been completed while others are under way.

Already the question of responsibility for high standards of quality of programed materials has been discussed by the organizations most directly concerned, and in the spring of 1961 a preliminary set of guide lines was established by a joint committee of the American Educational Research Association, the Department of Audio-Visual Instruction of the National Education Association, and the American Psychological Association. The final statement in the report is: "Active experimentation with self-instructional materials and devices is to be encouraged prior to large-scale adoption." Dr. Lloyd E. Homme, President of Teaching Machines Incorporated, and Dr. Allen Calvin, Director of the programing center of Encyclopedia Britannica Films, have both expressed the view that programs need to be tried out by the potential users. Calvin (1961) has strongly urged teachers *not* to be stampeded or to become too enthusiastic until they have cautiously investigated the characteristics and degree of effectiveness of any program that they are considering adopting for classroom use. Homme (1960) has pointed out that the only way to determine the effectiveness and appropriateness of a program is by having one or more students use it. The teacher can then determine, in any way he chooses, how well the student learned the content of the program. As Homme points out, an elaborate multiple-choice test is not necessary, for the teacher can ask questions which are as specific or as general as the objectives of the course require. The teacher can ask: "In what ways do a symphony and a concerto generally differ?" "What is meant by the 'Industrial Revolution'?" "What is a nuclear reactor, and how does it operate?" "Prove this theorem." A program cannot be evaluated fairly by skimming it the way we evaluate textbooks. A program that does not produce the desired terminal behavior is not adequate regardless of the extent to which it delights a teacher or programer. A program is only as good as the effectiveness with which it achieves its instructional objective, and this is true of any instructional device or technique. Obviously, the sooner the necessary experimentation and evaluation is accomplished, both in large group projects and in individual tryouts, the sooner the role of auto-instruction will be determined.

6

Teachers, Students, and Auto-Instruction

Introduction

*L*earning is a specific kind of change in the behavior patterns of an organism and is a never ending process, whether systematically guided and directed or left to chance encounters between the individual and his environment. A child learns from his parents, teachers, other adults, other children, and by himself; his behavior repertory is constantly changing, often to the dismay of his parents who never cease to be amazed at how much a child learns "accidentally," while apparently remaining impervious to the most intensive teaching efforts of home and school. A child is always learning but he is not always becoming educated, for education is a controlled and directed kind of learning, leading to a rather rigorously defined set of objectives. The responsibility for accomplishing these objectives lies with the teacher, who must know the specific directions in which learning is to be guided and must be able to provide appropriate guidance that will produce a change from "don't know" to "do know." In order to perform her tasks adequately a teacher must know about two activities: learning and teaching. Students preparing for a teaching career are usually required to take a searching

67

look at teaching methods and classroom practices, but they do not always learn systematically and adequately about the ways in which learning, retention, and forgetting take place. It is at least as important for a would-be teacher to know how students learn as it is for her to know how teachers teach.

We hope that our students will learn reasons for things rather than simply memorizing, copying, or parroting; we want them to understand "why" as well as "what." In similar fashion, teachers should understand the conditions under which learning occurs, the reasons why learning occurs when it does, and something about the extremely complicated ways in which teaching methods are related to the learning process. Unfortunately this knowledge, although necessary, is not sufficient by itself to permit a teacher to accomplish her objectives. The teacher's assignment is not a simple one, and the greater her motivation and desire to produce educated children the more frustrating is teaching likely to become due to the many obstacles that stand in her way.

The very structure of mass education in the United States imposes restrictions and limitations upon the teacher that often seem insurmountable. Consider a teacher who understands a great deal about the learning process and who is skilled in the performance of those manipulations called teaching. She understands the subject matter and the course objectives; she is highly motivated to succeed in adding something significant to the lives of her students; she is eager and excited about watching them grow in understanding and knowledge as they react to her and she to them. The group of students that she faces includes a wide range of ability, prior knowledge, interest, and motivation. She is responsible for seeing that each student learns, but the overwhelming number of students and the wide range of individual differences stand squarely in her path. If the teacher has only one student her effectiveness depends upon her ability to react in just the right way at just the right time to everything the student does. If there are two students she has to divide her attention between them, invariably reducing her effectiveness. For each additional student there is a further reduction in the individual attention she can provide and an inevitable decrement in the amount of learning that is produced. She attempts to involve the students in active consideration of the subject matter, but usually the system doesn't permit any but the most skillful teachers to do their jobs with any degree of the efficiency called for by the critical importances of the objectives of education. An eminent educator, appearing on television as a member of a panel discussing "The Crisis in Higher Education," made the sweeping statement that large lecture sections prove satisfactory only in the hands of the exceptional, inspired, and inspiring teacher who somehow knows how to get the students actively involved, and that in the hands of the average teacher a lecture presented to a large group accomplishes very little and might just as well be mimeographed rather than spoken.

Students need to produce ideas and try them out on their teachers and fellow students. Having students do this is rewarding to the teacher, but rarely does the opportunity exist for one of the slower students to produce an idea successfully in the classroom—his more capable classmates beat him to it. Then too, under the pressure of time the teacher may never be able to devote any attention to either individual or small group contacts for the purpose of discussing the implications, applications, and interesting sidelights of the subject matter, in which case the students really have little opportunity to deal with the content of their courses. Homework is one possible partial solution for the problems caused by classroom heterogeneity and the lack of manipulation of ideas, but there is more to it than this; contact between the teacher and the student accomplishes many things that are of importance to the student besides the clarification of ideas and the enrichment of the newly acquired knowledge. Personal contact and interaction permit the teacher to learn about the students, to know first hand how well each student is learning and to discover any existing personal or academic problems; further, the student learns more about the subject matter by seeing and following the teacher's own manipulation of ideas.

The basic obstacle confronting the teacher can be only partly eliminated by resectioning classes on the basis of intelligence, achievement, or academic aptitude. Each student needs more individual attention in the classroom in all of his contact with subject matter, both in learning the basic principles, definitions, concepts, and applications, and in dealing with it at a completely abstract and extrapolated level in the exchange of ideas with other persons. A teacher is rarely satisfied with being solely a lecturer, and the student often perceives the lecture class as being run by a rule of "stop thinking, be quiet, and listen." Unfortunately for both student and teacher the necessity for the teacher to spend much of her time lecturing, rewording the text, and forcing the students to pay attention to this kind of impersonal contact often results in the teacher becoming, in the eyes of her students, an authoritarian figure functioning merely as a talker, a tester, a grader, and a disciplinarian.

Suppose we give teachers additional time for personal contact with the students. Would that be of any help? It would, but a complete answer to this question obviously depends on where the time comes from. A teacher's working day is a full one and it usually extends into the hours after classes have ended. Teachers are expected to attend meetings with parents, act as advisors to scouts, music, art, science, dramatic and journalism organizations (to mention a few) and to sponsor an almost unlimited number of other extra-curricular activities. The teacher must also produce bulletin board displays and other visual decorations and assist in any worthwhile projects that can conceivably make school a more enjoyable and enriching experience. All of these time consuming activities are in addition to, and sometimes at the expense of, the more prosaic function of being responsible for the academic achievements of the students. Actually, the classroom time least well spent by the teacher is very likely the time that she spends doing the kind of teaching that auto-instruction can do much more effectively for her. If auto-instructional materials are used to relieve the teacher of one of the most ineffectual of her activities, she will have more time to spend doing the necessary things that she can do best for students. Auto-instruction will not necessarily make a teacher's job any easier, and might even make it more difficult, since the level of student achievement will be higher and the teacher must be prepared, skilled, and ready to talk about subject matter at a higher, more subtle, and more abstract level than present conditions require of her. A teacher will have to be a subject matter *expert* and will have to be prepared to deal with students who know more and are prepared to go further.

A common first reaction to auto-instruction by teachers and non-teachers alike is the mistaken idea that teaching machines were designed to replace teachers. There are few proponents of auto-instruction who seriously expect teachers to be eliminated and replaced by a machine or by a programed textbook; however, the statement has been made and most teachers will agree, that "any teacher replaceable by a machine deserves to be replaced." A very poor teacher will certainly be hopelessly lost and incapable of providing for students who are ready to go beyond the programs into guided "original thinking." The better teachers, on the other hand, will become even more irreplaceable than they are at present and auto-instruction will undoubtedly become a real teacher's pet because of the elimination of so much ineffective tedium.

THE STUDENT AND TEXTBOOKS

A weekly news magazine, in its education section, featured an article on auto-instruction which emphasized the inability of existing textbooks to proceed in appropriate small steps and to provide continuous reinforcement. In a letter to the editor a few issues later, a reader queried, "How did your education editor and Psychologist Skinner get so smart using the allegedly dull, inflexible, incomprehensible textbooks? And without the benefit of a programed learning machine?" This is a fair question, and in a broader sense becomes, "How *does* a reader learn by reading?" Undoubtedly he does so by some kind of "self-programing" in which the reader responds to the written material in covert fashion. That is, he considers a small amount of material, reacts to it, and either rereads it or continues on to the next statement. Corrective feedback is self-provided (e.g., "I don't understand"), and reinforcement probably occurs in the form of the student's being able to continue on to the subsequent material as well as in his realization that he is able to restate what he has just read. It is not implied that students do not learn from textbooks—they do. Some textbooks are easily evaluated as better written and more effective than others from the point of view of a student's ability to learn correctly from them. Part of the difference in textbook quality lies in the adequacy of the small step presentation of ideas and partly in the amount of covert responding that results from the student's reading of the material.

Auto-instruction will not replace books any more than it will replace teachers, since the ability to read and to learn by reading will always be an essential skill. Almost all programs, except for a few foreign language auditory presentation programs, require reading. Perhaps the reading skills produced as a non-specific consequence of experience with auto-instruction (non-specific in the sense of being beyond the specific subject matter content of a program) will transfer directly to improve the skill with which the student reads unprogramed printed matter. In other words, perhaps the kind of reading required by a program will gradually become a habitual method of reading unprogramed material more effectively: proceeding in small steps, paying close attention, dealing actively with the material, and being reinforced by the knowledge that understanding is developing. Whether or not positive transfer of this type can become a significant factor in the development of reading skills remains to be empirically determined, but in any event, auto-instruction does provide a new and unique research tool for the investigation of reading and the skills and behaviors of which it is composed. An occasional student can become somewhat over-dependent upon the efficiency of programed instruction and therefore must be weaned away to unprogramed material. Students demonstrating this difficulty tend to be those with already existent reading difficulties, and perhaps over-dependence is an inevitable result for poor readers because they have, probably for the first time, encountered a type of written material from which they too can learn.

In advising students having academic difficulties, teachers often suggest, and sometimes require, that the student learn to study by reading and outlining each paragraph in his own words. The objective here is the very kind of behavior that auto-instruction requires of the student every step of the way. If a student stops after reading a small bit of material, reacts to it, and repeats it in his own words, the over-all effect is that of self-programing. The reinforcement comes, as it does also in auto-instruction, when the student understands and knows that he understands what he has read. Often a student skims material, especially difficult material, by simply moving through the pages without comprehending very much of what he has read. This becomes strikingly evident when a poor reader, who has difficulty in comprehending anything at all from reading, "reads" at about the same rate of speed through materials of practically all levels of difficulty. That is, he may spend no more time on extremely difficult material than he does on only slightly difficult texts. Apparently he doesn't react to material that lies beyond his range of comprehension, and instead of stopping and going back when he loses track of the content and stops learning from it, he just reads on, picking up only the simple and obvious ideas—if he happens to pick up anything at all. A student using a program cannot skim in this manner and still be able to produce correct responses. The production of correct responses and the receiving of reinforcement result from, and in turn produce, comprehension and understanding. The student dealing with the frames in a program does not breeze through them without thought, without dealing with the content, or without having to make use of ideas in the production of responses. Some programs require only systematic attention to brief ideas and their application, but regardless of the specificity or generality of the behavior produced, all programs force the student to remain actively engaged and in contact with the subject matter.

Learning to read and to develop understanding from reading are skills that can be programed, and these skills will always be essential for dealing with material that must be read in the original unprogramed form. Although programed books will certainly replace many unprogramed books, the student will always have to do a considerable amount of reading of unprogramed material. The main characteristic of a program is the systematic learning that it produces. Books that consist primarily of aesthetically enriching material and topics for systematic analysis will remain unprogramed. Certainly no teaching machine enthusiast would suggest that the books that provide aesthetic enjoyment—plays, novels, expository material—should be programed. Programs contain material that is to be learned systematically—those concepts and principles which must be acquired by the student. Many kinds of literature must be read, understood, and learned *about,* but it is the descriptive supplementary material accompanying the literary work that is taught and which could be programed. A student doesn't become a scholar in the area of Shakespearean drama, for example, by memorizing the plays or even by memorizing the things that other people have said about them. Every college freshman or sophomore reads Shakespeare, but only guided reading, discussion, and active responding to the content results in anything more than a superficial acquaintance with his works.

Some kinds of subject matter—physics and mathematics for example—have already proven exceptionally appropriate for presentation in auto-instructional form while others have proven extremely difficult to the programer. Some subjects might prove to be inappropriate for auto-instruction and may need to be taught by a teacher dealing with very small discussion groups and using standard unprogramed text and reference books.

The Classroom

Many of the universally accepted and implemented theories that exist in present day education have grown out of a trial and error process of modifying education to meet the demands placed upon it. The resulting procedures are generally those that work best under existing conditions, although no educator would claim that our educational system is ideal and without serious problems. Following the launching of the first man-made satellite by the Soviet Union in 1957, exaggerated criticisms were hurled at the whole American educational structure by Americans who were, in many cases, unaware of any of the reasons why the structure exists in the form that it does or why its present problems have not simply been eliminated. Educators were aware of the problems long before the critical attention of the American public was focused on our school systems; however, the severe criticism has served a useful purpose—it did seem to make a greater number of educators, parents, politicians, and others directly and indirectly concerned with American schools increasingly aware of the fact that some rather sweeping innovations might be needed in order to modernize the classroom and to make it better equipped to meet the unceasing demand for a better education for more people.

The point has been made several times that teachers cannot deal adequately with large groups of students. The existing teacher shortage, along with the ever increasing number of students entering our schools each year, has resulted in the growth of class sizes while teacher-student contact has steadily decreased. Auto-instruction has obvious applications which can increase the teacher's personal contact with the students. At present, students in heterogeneous classes are individually penalized by the lack of systematic reinforcement and active involvement with subject matter. The students at the extreme upper and lower ends of the continuum of learning aptitude are usually additionally penalized because of the difference between the pace set by the teacher for the class and the rate of subject matter consideration that would be best for each individual student. The self-paced feature of auto-instruction (each student proceeding at his own rate) can at least partly eliminate the problem of the slower and faster learners who cannot adequately be taught by presentations designed for, and aimed more directly at the middle of the group.

Even beyond the advantages already noted, there are several possible effects of auto-instruction that could mean changes in the entire structure of the American educational system. Individual differences, which have been mentioned in relation to the fast and slow extremes of a heterogeneous group of students, have produced sectionings and assignment to "tracks" on the basis of ability (usually measured in terms of achievement and aptitude) as a partial replacement for the otherwise almost universal assignment to classes on the basis of chronological age. All five year old children are not ready for the first grade nor, necessarily, are all six year olds. If students with a wide range of mental ages and levels of social maturity are put together in the same classroom the difficulties confronting the teacher can become quite severe. If faster learners are permitted to skip grades some problems are partially solved while new problems are created. The differences in age, experience, strength, and so on, between a child who has skipped a grade and his new classmates can often produce serious emotional problems. A better solution is the use of special sections that meet only for certain classes in which students who are adequately prepared for, and capable of learning a specific course are put together regardless of their chronological ages or grade assignments. There is no reason why grade structures as we know them should be sacrosanct. Some children are held back and some are pushed too fast when they are assigned to grades and given exactly one school year in which to complete all of the courses assigned to that grade level. Each school year wastes a little of the better student's time—time that could be put to better use if the more capable student were permitted to move a little faster or further into each subject. The slower students, who do not quite have enough time in one school year, either fail and repeat the whole grade, spend the summer doing remedial work, or go on unprepared to the next grade where their probability of success is low before they begin, and where they fall even further behind.

Reassignment to groups or grades on any basis other than age or ability will also produce some kinds of problems. The difficulty is not in the grouping method used, but in assigning students to groups on any basis which does not permit individual attention appropriate to each student's current needs and levels of ability and preparation. The ideal—and this point was belabored earlier—would be to provide completely individual tutoring, one teacher for each student. The grouping of students into large classes did not originally occur in our schools because it was discovered to be the best of all possible methods, but because it was a reasonable and available substitute for tutoring. Certainly students will have to meet in groups in school for some purposes, and chronological age groupings have many advantages such as social contacts and personal friendships, and are probably necessary for courses such as physical education, for extra-curricular activities, and for any activity or situation in which chronological age is a significant factor. However, it makes little sense to retain such groupings if they can be replaced to the advantage of the student.

Skinner (1958) has suggested that the use of teaching machines might solve many of these problems by eliminating the rigidity of having to spend a fixed amount of time on a particular subject at a fixed period in the student's academic sequence, regardless of relevant individual differences. If programs are made available to students both for directed classroom study and for additional use as needed, no student will be held back by his classmates nor will he in any way restrict the rate at which others progress through the subject matter. A teacher can supervise a study period in a classroom in which dozens of students are working, each with his own machine or programed textbook, proceeding at his own rate in constant interaction with the program. The teacher's presence is required in order to prevent distractions, to provide personal guidance when requested, and to check frequently on the progress of the students—particularly those students who have severe academic difficulties. The students are free to consult the teacher whenever a problem arises (even the best of programs will contain an occasional frame that fails to communicate adequately with every student) or whenever the student's curiosity is aroused by something which is not elaborated upon in the program in sufficient detail to answer all of the questions that occur to him. A teacher can make use of auto-instruction in this manner or she can divide the class into small discussion groups which alternately use the programs and meet for discussions with her. She can even meet with the students individually for periodic tutorial contact. The possibilities are varied because of the flexibility that auto-instruction offers. Actually, like any other educational method, auto-instruction will have to be tried out in a variety of ways before the most appropriate kinds of applications can be specified. Limited experimental work is already being done to test some of these possibilities.

Teachers occasionally voice dissatisfaction with class groupings and the awkwardness of having to teach by lecturing to large groups of students. They are even more vociferous in expressing unfavorable opinions of grading systems and the use of grades to motivate students. Grades for course work are undesirable for many reasons: fear of failing or receiving a low grade can produce anxiety, and often hinders students rather than increasing their level of efficiency; grades often come to be perceived as the most important academic goals since honors, scholarships, "classroom fringe benefits" and many kinds of academic recognition seem to depend so much on a student's grade average; the teacher is forced to assign a single letter grade to a student, even though there are often many kinds of achievements that should be separately evaluated and recognized in a single course; and grades can also become the basis for a kind of reverse motivation in which the "gentleman's grade" of C becomes not only a rationalization for many students, but also the cause of better students lowering their sights and restricting their own level of achievement. Grades are considered to be, like heterogeneous groupings, a necessary evil accompanying mass education.

The possibility of doing away with both of these "necessary evils" has been suggested by Skinner (1958), who points out that auto-instruction might provide the wedge for dislodging many of the unsatisfactory features that keep modern education from becoming what it should be. In essence, Skinner's point concerning grades is that most letter grades indicate some degree of incompleteness of achievement. For example, a grade of C indicates incomplete but "average" acquisition of knowledge of the course content. The average student, and indeed most of the students, are two letter grades or more below the A level, and probably even A-quality achievement usually just barely escapes being incomplete to some degree. Incompleteness of achievement underlies all grading systems, including "grading on a curve," and the full responsibility for the incompleteness is awarded to the student along with the grade. We need not go into the inappropriateness of that point of view. Skinner suggests that if all students are able eventually to complete a program that reliably produces complete learning of the topic coverage, then an A could mean simply that a student had completed the program, a C could mean that he was perhaps half way through it, and so on. All students could eventually get an A in the course, assuming that the program really worked that well, so that letter grades would stop serving as motivating and anxiety-producing devices.

What will motivate students if grades no longer motivate or threaten? Very likely a student who is continually reinforced for making progress will continue to make progress and be motivated to continue to do so. The programs themselves provide this reinforcement by making the student aware of his progress at all times, and the teacher too will be a more liberal source of reinforcement in a more personal manner. A student is very likely to become bored if he dawdles and stops making progress, with the result that he will escape from boredom by moving on successfully to fresh material—another form of reinforcement that should affect the student's progress.

The complexities of recording achievement might not be successfully resolved by modifying grading systems in the way suggested tentatively by Skinner, and perhaps no single modification can be adequate. Here again the suggestions are interesting, if for no other reason than the fact that present practices *can* be modified and that auto-instruction suggests applications and methods that are testable.

One last point about the possible influence of auto-instruction on classroom practices concerns course work examinations. All students completing a program do not do equally well on an examination that directly tests knowledge of the program content. Some recognition must be made of these differences, and some students might do remedial work by redoing parts of the program where it seems to be necessary. This is another example of self-pacing, for although a student may have to proceed more slowly than his classmates he holds no one else back and he will eventually amass all of the course content. Tests will probably never be as traumatic when used to evaluate achievement from programs as they are when given to students who are pretty much on their own in preparing for a test. Mechner (1961) has pointed out that a test might even become necessary to convince the student that he really did learn as completely from the program as his progress indicates. Learning from a program is not effortless and is not passive, but the relative ease of moving through a well-written program with an appropriate progression of small steps may leave some students a bit worried about the lack of extreme difficulty in learning the material. Examples of this were cited in the preceding chapter. Imagine the novelty of taking a test for the primary purpose of showing yourself how much you *do* know rather than for the required purpose of letting someone else find out how much you do *not* know!

The possible effects of auto-instruction discussed in this chapter are only crude guesses concerning a few tentative applications of a still developing technology. Few of the hypothetical consequences have very much empirical support from actual classroom tryouts, but data of this sort are becoming available and have already been described in Chapter 5.

Auto-instruction is a new and promising development which promises to increase the effectiveness of mass education by offering individual instruction to all students more effectively than a teacher can do as long as the teacher is faced with the problem of producing learning in a large group of students all at the same time. Auto-instruction, if it lives up to its promise, can revolutionize education by providing the teacher with a more effective tool than any others that she has had at her disposal. Undeniably the poorer teachers—those who should not have been entrusted with the responsibilities of instruction in the first place—will not be able to keep up with students who demand more from them as a result of the uniformly thorough instruction provided by good programs. Of course, as programs become available in increasing variety and at various levels of complexity, teachers who would ordinarily take "refresher" or advanced courses at university and college summer schools could more economically pursue much of their continuing education via programs, and a large part of the teacher's work for advanced degrees could consist of work with programs, with only periodic course work requiring full-time attendance and interaction with other teachers enrolled in the same type of advanced course. There is no reason why education should not be both as effective and as human as possible, and far from dehumanizing or mechanizing education, auto-instruction should provide much greater opportunity for the student to come under the influence of the skilled human teacher than is currently possible.

BIBLIOGRAPHY

Barlow, J. A., "Conversational Chaining in Teaching Machine Programs," *Psychological Reports*, VII (1960).

Blyth, J. B., "Teaching Machines and Human Beings," (1960), in *Teaching Machines and Programmed Learning*, eds. A. A. Lumsdaine and R. Glaser. Washington, D.C.: Department of Audio-Visual Instruction, NEA, 1960.

Briggs, L. J., *A Survey of Cueing Methods in Education and in Automated Programs*. Pittsburgh: American Institute for Research, AIR-314-60-IR-106, 1960.

Calvin, A. D., Paper read at the American Psychological Association, New York, 1961.

Coulson, J. E. and H. F. Silberman, "Effects of Three Variables in a Teaching Machine." *Journal of Educational Psychology*, LI (1960).

Crowder, N. A., "Automatic Tutoring by Intrinsic Programming," in *Teaching Machines and Programmed Learning*, eds. A. A. Lumsdaine anl R. Glaser. Washington, D.C.: Department of Audio-Visual Instruction, NEA, 1960.

Dollard, J. and N. E. Miller, *Personality and Psychotherapy*. New York: McGraw-Hill Book Co., 1950.

Eigen, L. D. and P. K. Komoski, *Research Summary No. 1 of the Collegiate School Automatic Teaching Project*. New York, 1960.

Evans, J. L., R. Glaser, and L. E. Homme, *A Preliminary Investigation of Variations in the Properties of Verbal Learning Sequences of the "Teaching Machine" Type*. Paper read at Eastern Psychological Association, Atlantic City, 1959.

Feldhusen, J. A., "Reactions of College Students to a Self-Instructional Teaching Device and Programmed Instruction," *AID*, I (1961).

Ferster, C. B. and S. M. Sapon, "An Application of Recent Developments in Psychology to the Teaching of German," *Harvard Educational Review*, XXVIII (1958).

Fry, E. B., "A Study of Teaching Machine Response Modes" (1960), in *Teaching Machines and Programmed Learning*, eds. A. A. Lumsdaine and R. Glaser. Washington, D.C.: Department of Audio-Visual Instruction, NEA, 1960.

Galanter, E., ed., *Automated Teaching: The State of the Art*. New York: John Wiley & Sons, Inc., 1959.

Gilbert, T. F., "On the Relevance of Laboratory Investigation of Learning to Self-Instructional Programming" (1959), in *Teaching Machines and Programmed Learning*, eds. A. A. Lumsdaine and R. Glaser. Washington, D.C.: Department of Audio-Visual Instruction, NEA, 1960.

Glaser, R., L. E. Homme, and J. L. Evans, "An Evaluation of Textbooks in Terms of Learning Principles" (1959), in *Teaching Machines and Programmed Learning*, eds. A. A. Lumsdaine and R. Glaser. Washington, D.C.: Department of Aulio-Visual Instruction, NEA, 1960.

Goldbeck, R. A. and L. J. Briggs, *An Analysis of Response Mode and Feedback Factors in Automated Instruction*. Technical Report No. 2, Santa Barbara: American Institute for Research, 1960.

Guthrie, E. R., *The Psychology of Learning*. New York: Harper and Brothers, Publishers, 1952.

Harlow, H. W., "The Nature of Love," *American Psychologist*, XIII (1958).

Homme, L. E., Personal communication, 1961.

―――― and D. J. Klaus, *Laboratory Studies in the Analysis of Behavior*. Pittsburgh: Lever Press, 1957.

―――― and R. Glaser, *Problems in Programming Verbal Learning Sequences*. Paper read at the American Psychological Association, Cincinnati, 1959.

Holland, J. G., *Teaching Psychology by a Teaching Machine Program*. Paper read at the American Psychological Association, Cincinnati, 1959.

――――, *Design and Use of a Teaching Machine Program*. Paper read at the American Psychological Association, Chicago, 1960.

―――― and B. F. Skinner, *The Analysis of Behavior*. New York: McGraw-Hill Book Co., Inc., 1961.

――――, Personal communication, 1961.

Hosmer, C. L. and J. A. Nolan, "Time Saved by a Tryout of Automatic Tutoring," *Automated Teaching Bulletin*, I (1960).

Keller, F. S. and W. N. Schoenfeld, *Principles of Psychology*. New York: Appleton-Century-Crofts, Inc., 1950.

Klaus, D. J., "Programming—the Tutorial Approach," *Audio-Visual Instruction*, VI (1961).

――――, "The Art of Auto-Instructional Programming," *AV Communication Review*, IX (1961).

―――― and A. A. Lumsdaine, *Some Economic Realities of Teaching Machine Instruction*. Paper read at the American Psychological Association, Chicago, 1960.

―――― and ――――, *An Experimental Field Test of the Value of Self-Tutoring Materials in High School Physics: An Interim Report of Progress and Preliminary Findings*. Pittsburgh: American Institute for Research, 1960.

―――― and ――――, *Increased Learning from TV Courses by Use of Integrated Self-Instructional Quiz Materials anl "Practice Machines."* Progress report submitted to the U. S. Office of Education. Pittsburgh: American Institute for Research, January 30, 1961.

―――― and W. A. Deterline, *Student Reactions to Auto-Instruction*. Pittsburgh: American Institute for Research, in preparation.

Lumsdaine, A. A. and R. Glaser, eds., *Teaching Machines and Programmed Learning*. Washington, D.C.: Department of Audio-Visual Instruction, NEA, 1960.

Lysaught, J., ed., *Programmed Learning: Evolving Principles and Industrial Applications.* Ann Arbor: Foundation for Research on Human Behaviors, 1961.

Mechner, F., *Programming for Automated Instruction.* Unpublished paper (mimeo), 1961.

Porter, D., "Teaching Machines," *Harvard Graduate School of Education Association Bulletin,* III (1958).

Pressey, S. L., "A Third and Fourth Contribution Toward the Coming 'Industrial Revolution' in Education." *School and Society,* XXXVI (1932).

————, "Development and Appraisal of Devices Providing Immediate Automatic Scoring of Objective Tests and Concomitant Self-Instruction," (1950), in *Teaching Machines and Programmed Learning,* eds. A. A. Lumsdaine and R. Glaser. Washington, D.C.: Department of Audio-Visual Instruction, NEA, 1960.

Roe, A., "Five Teaching Methods Tested at UCLA Department of Engineering," Research Note, *AID,* I (1961).

————, M. Massey, G. Weltman, and D. Leeds, *Automated Teaching Methods Using Linear Programs.* Department of Engineering, University of California, Los Angeles, Report No. 50-105, 1960.

Silverman, R. E., *The Use of Context Cues in Teaching Machines.* Technical Report NAVTRADEVCEN 507-1. Port Washington, New York: U. S. Naval Training Devices Center, 1960.

Skinner, B. F., *Science and Human Behavior.* New York: Macmillan Co., 1953.

————, "The Science of Learning and the Art of Teaching," *Harvard Educational Review,* XXIV (1954).

————, "Teaching Machines," *Science,* CXXVIII (1958).

————, "Learning Theory and Future Research." Paper delivered at Ann Arbor, 1960, in *Programmed Learning: Evolving Principles and Industrial Applications,* ed. J. Lysaught. Ann Arbor: Foundation for Research on Human Behaviors, 1961.

———— and J. G. Holland, *The Use of Teaching Machines in College Instruction.* Final report to The Fund for the Advancement of Education, 1958.

Stolurow, L. M., *Teaching by Machine.* Washington, D.C.: U. S. Government Printing Office, 1961.

Thorndike, E. L., *Animal Intelligence: Experimental Studies.* New York: Macmillan, 1911.

————, *The Original Nature of Man (Educational Psychology, I).* New York: Teachers College, 1913.

Appendix

INSTRUCTIONS

This appendix contains a brief presentation of some ideas that are related to tests and test interpretation. It differs from most written material in that it is broken down into small segments, and you will have to answer a simple question about each segment before going on to the next segment. Each part of this appendix is written a bit differently. When you turn to the next page you will find the first segment. Read it and then answer the multiple-choice question at the end of the segment by putting a checkmark beside your choice, but then do *not* turn to page 2: instead, look at the page number beside the answer that you checked and turn directly to that page, and read either the top or bottom half of that page depending on where you were told to look. For example, on page 1 there are three choices. If you select the first choice you will be told to turn to the *top* of page 2. If you select the second choice you will be told to go to the bottom of page 7, and so on. Be sure to note both the page number and whether you are to read the top or bottom half of the page. If you chose the correct answer, the new page will tell you that you were correct and will then explain the next segment. If you made an error you will be told that you were wrong and why your choice was incorrect. You will then be told to return to the page on which you made an error and to try again to pick out the correct choice.

Scores on a test are usually referred to as "raw" scores, and each raw score is simply the number of correct answers. A raw score of 34 means that a certain student answered 34 questions correctly. A percentage score is slightly different, since a raw score of 34 could mean 100%, or 50%, or any percentage between 1 and 100. If there were only 34 items on the test, a raw score of 34 would be 100% correct, and if there were 68 items on the test, a raw score of 34 would be 50% correct. A percentage is easily calculated by dividing the raw score by the total number of items on the test. If a raw score of 15 is 25% correct, how many questions were there on the test? 60, of course. If there were 30 items on the test, and the highest score is 27 items correct, and the lowest raw score is 15, the highest raw score is what percentage correct?

If your answer is: Turn to:

27%   page 2, top half of the page
81%   page 7, bottom half of the page
90%   page 11, bottom half of the page

From page 1

Your answer, 27%, is wrong. Remember that 27 is the raw score, which is simply a count of the number of correct answers. To find a percentage you must ask—27 is what percentage of 30? To get the answer, you simply write the question this way : $27 \div 30 = ?$; by dividing 27 by 30 you get the correct answer. Go back to page 1 and work out the correct answer.

From page 20

Your answer was H + L + 1. There's one plus sign in there that should be a minus sign. Look at this example. H = 10, L = 4. You wouldn't say that the range is $10 + 4 + 1 = 15$, would you? O.K., turn back to the bottom of page 20, and watch the plus and minus signs.

From page 9

Your answer was 6 out of 20 is 30%, and you are correct, of course. In other words, in this set of scores:

8, 9, 9, 10, 11, 11, 11, 12, 12, 13, 14, 15, 15, 16, 17, 17, 18, 19, 20, 21

a score of 16 is surpassed by only 30% of the scores. Now, if 30% of the scores are above 16, then the difference between 30% and 100% represents the percentage of scores equal to or lower than a score of 16. That is, the percentage of scores in this set of scores *equal to* or *lower than* a score of 16 is:

30%	5	bottom
65%	14	top
70%	7	top

From page 12

You feel that a score of 22/25 (88% correct) is a poor score. It might be, but it might be a very good score! If it happened to be the highest score ever achieved on a very difficult test, it would be a pretty good score, wouldn't it? You see, you can't really tell very much about a score unless you know something about the test and about the other scores. Turn to the bottom of page 12 and admit you can't tell much from the information that was given.

From page 7

You said that in a group of 5 scores, the 2nd score from the top has a percentile rank of 80. You're right. That score would be called the 80th percentile. Remember, a percentile does not indicate the percentage of correct answers, it represents the percentage of test scores falling at or below that score. Now look at this set of scores:

7, 8, 8, 9, 10, 10, 10, 11, 11, 12, 13, 14, 14, 15, 15, 15, 16, 17, 17, 18, 19, 19, 19, 20, 20

There are 25 scores. There were 45 test items. Three students scored 15. Now be careful with this question: a raw score of 15 is what percentage correct, and what percentile rank?

30 per cent correct, 52nd percentile	page 10 bottom
64 per cent correct, 33rd percentile	page 8 bottom
33 per cent correct, 64th percentile	page 14 bottom
15 per cent correct, 36th percentile	page 17 top

From page 11

Your answer was 19. You're correct.

You could determine the range by counting, 11, 12, 13 and so on, from the lowest score of 11, to the highest score, which is 29, but there is an easier and faster way. Our other example was lowest score is 6 and highest score is 9. The range is four—6, 7, 8 and 9, and notice that the highest score minus the lowest is 3, one less than the range. We can't say that 9 minus 6 is the range because 9 minus 6 leaves only 3 numbers, and the range includes 4 numbers. To sum up all of these remarks we can say that the range is equal to:

the highest score minus the lowest score plus one	16 top
the highest score minus the lowest score	10 top
the highest score plus the lowest score	13 bottom

From page 16

Your answer was 11. To get that answer you would have to subtract the lowest score from the highest and then stop at that point—you didn't add 1—remember? Go back to the top of page 16 and do the *whole* procedure this time.

From page 3

30% *above* 16 could not possibly leave only 30% *below* and *equal to* a score of 16. 100% minus 30% does not leave 30%. The right answer is shown at the top of page 3, go back and pick it out.

From page 11

You said that the range is 18 when the highest score is 29 and the lowest is 11. You went wrong and came up with the wrong answer because you simply subtracted 11 from 29. Go back and read page 11 again, particularly the example of 6 to 9. Notice, that 9 — 6 is 3, but the range is 4. Begin to see the point? O.K., go on now to the bottom of page 4.

From page 12

You said that a raw score of 22 correct from a total of 25, which is 88% correct, is a good score. Not necessarily! Suppose everyone else in the group who took the test received a score of 25—100%. For example, suppose a class of college students was told "The first letter of the alphabet is A. Write down the other 25 letters." Would you really call a score here of 88% a "good" score? You see, you can't tell much from a raw score or a percentage even if you know that the test was appropriate for those students. Now go back to the bottom of page 12 and admit that you can't tell much from the information that was given.

From page 3

You said that since 30% of the scores are above 16, there must be 70% at or below a score of 16. That's right. A score of 16 is said to have a percentile rank of 70%. A percentile, or the percentile rank of a score, is the percentage of scores that fall *at* or *below* that score. In this set of scores, what is the percentile rank of a score of 66?

$$51, \ 62, \ 63, \ 66, \ 72$$

80th percentile	4 top
20th percentile	9 bottom
66th percentile	12 top

From page 1

Your answer, 81%, is wrong, but how did you come up with this answer? Was it just a guess, or did you multiply 27 by 30 and then misplace a decimal point? In any case, you simply want to know what percentage of 30 a score of 27 represents. To find out, you divide the score by the total, that is, divide 27 by 30. When you do that you find that 27 is what percentage of 30? Go back to page 1 and select the correct answer.

From page 18

Very good. This wasn't the right answer, of course, but your curiosity is to be commended. When a reader comes upon an unfamiliar word like "gazornenplatt" (which is not a real word by the way), he should be curious and alert enough to look it up. This was not really meant to trick you, but to commend those of you who were motivated enough to turn to this page to see what the word means. Now go on back to the bottom of page 18 and pick out the right answer.

From page 4

Both of your answers are incorrect! Now remember that per cent correct is the score divided by the total number of questions. The percentile rank on the other hand refers to percentage of scores, not percentage of questions. Percentile rank of a score at 15 is the percentage of scores falling at or below 15. O.K., now keep those two things clear and go back to the top of page 4 and work out the correct answers.

From page 20

Your answer was R = H — L + 1. That's right. The highest score minus the lowest score plus 1. Usually, in addition to knowing the range, you want to know something about each score, whether it is the highest, the lowest, right in the middle, in the upper third, and so on. A useful method of indicating something about each score is to report the position of the score compared to all other scores. If we count the number of scores that fall above a particular score we can see how many students score higher. For example, look at these scores: 8, 9, 9, 10, 11, 11, 11, 12, 12, 13, 14, 15, 15, 16, 17, 17, 18, 19, 20, 21. There are 20 scores. Look at the score of 16. Only 6 students score higher than 16. Now, out of the 20 students, what percentage of those 20 were higher than 16?

20%	17 bottom
30%	3 top
65%	19 bottom

From page 7

Your answer of 20% was much too low! There were 5 scores—51, 62, 63, 66 and 77—and of these scores, 4 of them fall at or below 66. What is the percentile rank of 66 if 4 out of 5 scores fall at or below 66? You simply divide 4 by 5, which gives you the percentage of scores at or below 66, and that percentage is called a percentile rank. Now go back to page 7, at the top, and pick out the right percentile rank.

From page 4

You said highest minus lowest. Wrong! What were you doing when you were supposed to be reading the material at the bottom of page 4? The range is *not* simply the highest minus the lowest score. Don't be in too much of a hurry. If you read carefully you can move through the material faster. Just be sure you know the correct answer before you turn a page—don't guess. Now go back to the bottom of page 4 and try again.

From page 4

You said 30% correct, and the 52nd percentile; both are wrong! Here's a hint—for per cent correct divide the raw score by the total number of questions. To get the percentile, divide the scores at or below 15 by the total number of scores. Remember, a percentage has to do with the number of test items, and a percentile refers to the number of scores. Now go back to the top of page 4 and work it out again.

From page 15

You said 5 students received scores of 7, but you miscounted. Go back to the top of page 15, locate the number 7 under the blocks, and count the number of blocks above the number 7.

From page 1

You said 90%, which is correct since 27 divided by 30 = .90, or 90%. A raw score of 27 correct out of 30 is equivalent to a percentage score of 90%. If 7 students take a test, and 2 receive a score of 6, 2 a score of 7, 1 a score of 8, and 2 a score of 9, we have a lowest score of 6 and highest score of 9. How many possible different scores are there between 6 and 9, *inclusive?* There are 4 possible scores—6, 7, 8 and 9. The total number of possible scores is called the range. If the highest score is 29 and the lowest score is 11, what is the range?

18   page 6 top
19   page 4 bottom

From page 7

66% could not possibly be the right answer no matter how you calculated. You must have been guessing. Go back to the top of page 7 and read it again, then work out the answer.

From page 14

You have now learned what is meant by a raw score, a percentage score, a percentile, and the range of a set of scores. What does a raw score, or a percentage score tell you about a student? For example, suppose a student receives a raw score of 22 out of 25, which is 88% correct; this is a:

good score	page 6 bottom
poor score	page 3 bottom
can't tell	page 15 top

From page 15

You said 6 students received a score of 7, but there are not 6 blocks above the number 7. Go back to the top of page 15 and count the blocks above the number 7.

From page 4

You chose the highest score plus the lowest score, which is incorrect. If the highest score is 30 and the lowest score is 28, by adding them you'd get a total of 58, and that's not a reasonable range for 28 to 30 is it? Now turn back to the bottom half of page 4 and make the correct choice.

From page 3

You chose 65% as the correct answer, but you've overlooked part of the instructions. If you count only the scores *below* 16, you'll find 65% of the scores, but we want to know the percentage falling *at or below* 16, that is, you must count the score of 16 also. If 30% fall above 16, then all the rest of the scores must fall *at or below* 16. 100% minus 30% equals the right answer. Go back to the top of page 3 and pick that answer.

From page 4

Your answer—15 correct out of 45 is 33%, which is correct, and 15 has a percentile rank of 64, which is also correct. Now determine the percentile rank for these three scores: 10, 17, and 19.

7, 8, 8, 9, 10, 10, 10, 11, 11, 12, 13, 14, 14, 15, 15, 15, 16, 17, 17, 18, 19, 19, 19, 20, 20.

Write the percentile ranks here:

Raw score	Percentile
10	_____
17	_____
19	_____

Now, without losing your place on this page, turn to the top of page 20 and compare the percentiles you just wrote with the correct answers shown there, then continue reading the rest of the top of page 20.

From page 12

You said you can't tell, and you're right; unless you are arbitrarily going to say "Anything less than perfect (100%) is a poor score," or anything above, say 80%, is a good score. Ordinarily, an absolute judgment of this sort is risky, and you should consider not only the percentage correct, but the relative position of all of the scores. If 80% is the lowest score in a set of scores, the student who scored 80% is less proficient than any other student in the group. There are several ways, in addition to percentile ranks, in which a set of scores can be evaluated, and in order to understand these methods, we must first look at certain characteristic sets of scores. In this figure, each block represents one student. Notice that only one student received a score of 3, six students received a score of 5 and how many received a score of 7?

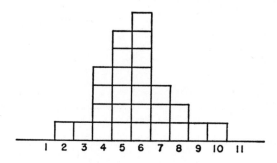

3	STUDENTS	18	BOTTOM
5	STUDENTS	11	TOP
6	STUDENTS	13	TOP

From page 18

A square, you said. No, the shape would be higher in the center, tapering off at the ends, and would resemble a bell. Now turn directly to page 21.

From page 4

Your answer was the highest score minus the lowest score plus one. That's right. If the highest score is 23 and the lowest score is 12, the range is equal to:

23   page 18 top
11   page 5 top
12   page 20 bottom

From page 18

You said that the shape of the distribution would resemble the letter V. Well, if the V is rightside up, that would indicate a piling up of scores at the two ends, with very few in the middle, which is exactly the opposite of the usual findings. If you turn the V upside down (Λ), it looks a bit more like the proper shape. However, the best answer is that the distribution would most closely resemble a bell, high in the middle, sloping down on each side to the bottom. Now turn to page 21.

From page 4

You've made a mistake. Turn to the bottom of page 8 and read it carefully.

From page 9

You chose a wrong answer—20%. Let's take a look at the steps involved in arriving at the answer. The question was, what percentage scored *above* 16. The scores above 16 were 17, 17, 18, 19, 20, 21, a total of 6 scores out of 20. To find the percentage you divide 6 by 20, and get what? Go back to the bottom of page 9 and choose the correct answer.

From page 16

You misread the question. You said the range is 23, which is the wrong answer. The highest score is 23 and the lowest is 12, so the range is all of the possible scores from 12 to 23, which couldn't be 23, could it? Go back to the top of page 16 and work out the right answer.

From page 15

You read the figure correctly, counting three blocks at a score of 7. The scores in that figure were not evenly distributed throughout the range; there was a tendency for scores to pile up in the center, with very few scores at the bottom and at the top. From the last sentence we can put several words together to describe this characteristic: a distribution (set) of scores typically shows a central tendency of concentration. "Central tendency" refers to the piling up of scores in the middle of the distribution. This means that if we make a graph of a distribution, just like the one you just saw, with one block for each student, the shape of the distribution would most resemble:

a square	15 bottom
a bell	21 top
the letter V	16 bottom
a gazornenplatt	8 top

From page 20

You said H — L, but how could you? You forgot one very, very important detail. Where is the 1 that you are supposed to add on? Go back to the bottom of page 20 and this time don't forget the 1 you missed.

From page 9

Your answer, 65%, would have been correct if the question had been different, but the question read: What percentage of scores fall *above* 16. There were 6 scores above 16—17, 17, 18, 19, 20 and 21—and to find the percentage you divide 6 by 20, since there were 20 scores. Go ahead, divide and then go back to the top of page 9 and pick out the correct answer.

From page 14

Raw Score	Percentile
10	28th
17	76th
19	92nd

If *all three* of your answers were correct, turn now to the bottom of page 12. If you made any errors, work on the problem again until you get the correct answer shown above. Here is the set of scores:

7, 8, 8, 9, 10, 10, 10, 11, 11, 12, 13, 14, 14, 15, 15, 15, 16, 17, 17, 18, 19, 19, 19, 20, 20.

Raw score of 10—

Remember count all the scores at and below 10. This adds up to 7 scores, which you divide by 25, and get what? _____

Raw score of 17—

There are 17 scores below 17 and 2 scores of 17—a total of 19 scores at or below 17. 19 divided by 25 is what? _____

Raw score of 19—

There are 25 scores altogether, 2 of them above 19, and 23 at or below 19. 23 divided by 25 is what? _____

When you have corrected your errors, turn to the bottom of page 12.

From page 16

If the highest score is 23 and lowest is 12, the range is 12. If R = range, H = highest score, and L = lowest score, it is possible to write a formula for determining the range. The formula is written:

$$R = H + L + 1 \qquad \text{page 2 bottom}$$
$$R = H - L \qquad \text{page 19 top}$$
$$R = H - L + 1 \qquad \text{page 9 top}$$

From page 18

Of course—the shape of the distribution would most resemble a bell, and a distribution of scores is often described as a "bell-shaped" curve. Many kinds of measures—not only test scores—tend to distribute themselves in a bell-shaped curve. If we measure the height or weight of 100 students, all of the same age and sex, we generally find very few very tall or very heavy students, and very few very short or very light students. Within the range of measurements, most cluster near the center, with only a few at the extremes. You are now going to learn some of specific descriptions and interpretations that make up what is called "descriptive statistics." Remember, you have already learned that the Range = H — L + 1, and that a percentile rank of a score is the percentage of scores that fall at or below that score. A percentile is one kind of statistic, and the other statistics you are going to learn about are not much more complicated than percentiles. When you turn to page 23 you will find the beginning of a set of frames. In each frame you will find one or more blanks. You will be able to fill in each blank, either because the correct answer is made clear by the frame, or because you learned it in preceding frames. A single blank like this _____ means you are to fill in just one word. When you find a larger blank with an asterisk (*) in it like this *_____, you are to use more than one word, usually a specific set of words or a "pat phrase." When a blank contains two asterisks like this **_____, use your own words; don't try to remember only one way of writing the answer. If a number is required, the blank will look like this, (#) _____, while a blank that looks like this (s) _____ calls for a symbol, letter, abbreviation or formula.

Now, following the directions you just read, *fill in the following blanks.* In this first blank, write in #_____ number, and in this next blank write in one _____. A single asterisk (*) means you must write in more than *_____, and a double asterisk means that **_____. You don't need to be shown the answers to these blanks, since, if necessary, you can find them by reading the preceding paragraph. You have seen how a branching program might look. The next portion of the program is a constructed response series of short frames. Later in the program you will encounter a combination of other kinds of frames. The frames in the following pages are laid out in a special way, with only five frames on each page. Do *not* read the frames one after another down the page as you ordinarily do when reading a page in a book. You must follow the frames by number from one page to the next. Frame 1 appears on the next page, but frame 2 does not; it appears on the top of the following page, then frame 3 at the top of the page after that, and so on. You are to read the top frame on each page until you come to a page telling you to return to this page, and then you are to read the second frame on this next page, then the second frame on the following page, and so on again to the return page. Be sure to follow the same row of frames from one page to the next until you arrive at the page that tells you to come back and start on a new row of frames. Not all programed textbook arrangements of frames follow this form; sometimes the frames are in sequence on the right hand pages, requiring that the book be turned around so the student can work back toward the beginning of the book; in another kind of arrangement the frames simply follow each other in sequence on the same page—you will encounter that kind of arrangement later on in this program. In this next part of the program you will find the correct answer to each frame printed beside the following frame. Now, to get back to the subject of the program—statistics—go on to frame 1.

1. Graphs and tables look complex, but they can help you picture relationships between students and their test scores. Let's review the things you have learned about graphs of scores. Frequency means number of times. If four students receive the same score on a test, that score has a _____ of four.

---

12. higher (better)
    lower (poorer)
    scores

13. To discriminate means "tell the difference." A test must detect differences between students, that is, it must _____ between students.

---

24. can not rely on
    the scores

25. An unreliable measurement or score is not trustworthy. We can have confidence in a _____ measurement, but not in an _____ measurement.

---

36. valid measure
    intelligence

37. Test validity refers to a tests's effectiveness in _____ what it was designed to _____.

---

48. predict
    aptitude

49. A test used to evaluate past learning is called an *_____ while a test used for prediction is called an *_____.

1. frequency

2. If 20 students receive a score of 23 on a test, a score of 23 has a _____ of #_____.

---

13. discriminate

14. A test must be able to _____ between students. If all students receive the same score on a test, the test **_____.

---

25. reliable
    unreliable

26. If Johnny takes the same test 3 times, and gets 3 very different scores, the _____ is not reliable, and neither is any one of the 3 _____.

---

37. measuring
    measure

38. Validity and reliability are two characteristics of a good test. Validity means the extent to which a test *_____

_____.

---

49. achievement
    test
    aptitude test

50. We call a test an achievement test or an aptitude test depending on how we use it. It is called an achievement test if we use it to **_____.

2. frequency
   20

---

3. Very few students get the highest scores and very few get the _____ scores. Very high and very low scores have small or low _____.

---

14. discriminate
    does not dis-
    criminate
    (between stu-
    dents)

---

15. Students do not all receive exactly the _____ score if the test successfully _____ differences in their knowledge.

---

26. test
    scores

---

27. An unreliable test doesn't tell us very much, because a student might get a much _____ or _____ score if he took the test again.

---

38. measures what
    it is supposed
    (was de-
    signed) to
    measure

---

39. If a test is designed to measure knowledge of history, but tests only memory for dates, it is probably not a *_____ of knowledge of history.

---

50. measure how
    much a stu-
    dent has
    achieved
    (learned) etc.

---

51. We call a test an aptitude test if we use it to **_____ _____.

3. lowest
frequencies

4. In this figure, each block represents one student. The score with the highest frequency is #_____, while 12 has the *_____.

TEST SCORE

---

15. same
discriminates

16. Although students should not all receive the same score, students with equal knowledge should receive *_____.

---

27. higher
lower

28. If we know that a test is reliable, we can rely on test scores and assume that if the student took the test again his **_____.

---

39. valid test (valid measurement)

40. If students who know nothing about biology can figure out the answers to a biology test by their sentence structure, the test is not **_____
_____.

---

51. predict something about the future (future performance)

52. A test may be either an *_____ or an *_____, depending on **_____.

4. 8 lowest (small- est) frequency (frequency of one)	5. Frequency means the _____ of times. In the figure on the right, a score of # _____ has the highest frequency since that score oc- curs the greatest *_____.
16. equal scores (the same score)	17. A test is a measuring instrument, and a test must be accurate and consistent, like any good _____ instrument. A test must correctly _____ differences between students.
28. score would be approximately the same (score would not change much, etc.)	29. We can have confidence in a score on a reliable test because **_____ _____.
40. a valid test of knowledge of biology	41. "Tall people are more intelligent than shorter people" is untrue. Height is not a *_____ of _____.
52. aptitude test achievement test how it is used (whether we use it to meas- ure part learn- ing or to pre- dict, etc.)	53. Regardless of whether a test is an achievement test or an aptitude test it must be _____, _____ and must be able to **_____ _____.

5. number
17
number of
times

6. The frequency with which a score occurs means the *_____ that score occurs. A frequency of 16 means that **_____
_____.

17. measuring
discriminate
(detect)

18. A ruler is a _____ instrument which measures length, or distance; we would _____ use a ruler to measure weight.

29. the score would
not change
much if the
student takes
the test again,
etc.

30. A test must detect differences between students, that is, it must _____ between students who have _____ levels of achievement.

41. valid measure
intelligence

42. A test can be reliable without being valid. A tape measure is not a _____ of intelligence, but the measures can be _____.

53. reliable
valid
discriminate
(detect) dif-
ferences be-
tween stu-
dents

54. A test can be _____ even though it might not measure what it is supposed to measure, that is, without being _____.

6. number of
   times
   a score of 16
   occurred 16
   times (or, 16
   students got
   that score)

7. We describe a group of scores as making up a distribution. Any group of scores from lowest to highest makes up a _____ of scores.

18. measuring
    not

19. A ruler made of rubber would be of little use because we could not rely on any _____ taken with it.

30. discriminate
    different

31. Reliability means the degree to which a test makes consistent discriminations. A test must make *_____ or we can't rely on it.

42. valid
    reliable

43. If a test is reliable its discriminations are dependable, but the test is not valid unless it ** _____ .

54. reliable
    valid

55. Validity means ** _____
_____ .

7. distribution

8. Frequency means *_____. A graph that shows the frequency with which each score occurs is called a frequency _____.

---

19. measurement (measure)

20. If we can *rely* on a measuring device, we say that it is reliable. A rubber ruler is not a _____ measuring instrument.

---

31. consistent discriminations

32. If a test is _____ in its discriminations it is a _____ test, but if it is unreliable, it is not *_____.

---

43. measures what it is supposed to measure

44. Tests are used for many purposes. An achievement test is used to measure a student's _____ in a course.

---

55. the extent to which a test measures what it is supposed to measure

56. A test that does not discriminate consistently cannot accurately measure what it is supposed to measure, which means a test cannot be _____ _____ unless it is _____.

8. number of
   times
   distribution

9. Distributions of scores that show the number of times each score occurred are called *_____ _____.

---

20. reliable

21. A rubber ruler used to measure the width of this book would give many wrong _____ because a rubber ruler is not a _____ measuring device.

---

32. consistent
    reliable
    consistent in its
    discrimina-
    tions

33. Reliability means **_____ _____ _____.

---

44. achievement

45. A test which evaluates past learning by measuring present performance is called an _____ test; it is a _____ of how much each student has _____.

---

56. valid
    reliable

57. A test can be _____ without being _____, but cannot be **_____ _____.

9. frequency distributions	10. This bell shaped curve shows the typical shape of most *_____. In the middle of the _____ the _____ are higher than at the extremes. FREQUENCY (NUMBER OF STUDENTS) TEST SCORE
21. measurements reliable	22. If we measure the same thing several times with a _____ measuring device, we will get approximately the _____ measurement each time.
33. the extent to which a test makes consistent discriminations	34. A valid test measures what it is supposed to measure. A test that doesn't measure what it is said to measure is not a _____ test.
45. achievement test measure (test) achieved (learned)	46. Most of the tests that a teacher deals with are _____ tests, which measure **_____ _____.
57. reliable valid valid without being reliable (valid unless it is reliable)	58. A test which accurately and consistently measures achievement is a _____ and _____ achievement test.

10. frequency dis-
    tributions
    distribution
    frequencies

11. When students take a test, you expect the students who know more about the subject to get _____ scores than students who know less.

22. reliable
    same

23. If you are told that a book is 11 inches wide, as measured by a rubber ruler, you would _____ consider the measurement to be _____.

34. valid

35. A ruler is a _____ measure of distance, but a ruler is _____ a *_____ _____ of weight.

46. achievement
    how much a
    student has
    learned
    (achieved)

47. Tests are sometimes used to predict future performance. A test always measures present performance, but sometimes can be used to _____ something about the future.

58. valid
    reliable

59. Frequency means *_____. A graph showing the frequencies of a set of scores is called a *_____.

11. higher (better)	12. The purpose of a test is to discriminate between students so that better students get ＿＿＿＿ scores and poorer students get *＿＿＿＿ ＿＿＿＿.
23. not reliable	24. If a test is reliable you can rely on the scores, but if a test is unreliable, you *＿＿＿＿ ＿＿＿＿.
35. valid not valid measure	36. An "intelligence test" that measures only knowledge of French is not a *＿＿＿＿ of ＿＿＿＿.
47. predict	48. A test used to ＿＿＿＿ something about future performance is called an aptitude test. A test which predicts success or failure in college is a college ＿＿＿＿ test.
59. number of times frequency distribution	60. You are now going to go on to a new set of frames, arranged in a different way. Turn the next page and go on to the next part of the program.

When you reach this page return to page 23 and begin the next row of items.

61. From here on, read the entire page before turning to the next page. Fill in every blank as before. The correct answers appear in the right hand margin, so take a sheet of paper or cardboard and cover the correct answers so that you will not be tempted to look at them before you have filled in the blanks. After filling in a blank, slide the paper down until you can see the correct answer. In some cases the correct answer will not be shown, but you will be told where to find it. Follow all directions carefully. Now, before going on, get a piece of paper or cardboard and use it to ** _____ | If you aren't
_____ | sure of this
_____ . | answer, read the
| frame again.

62. Sometimes a single number can tell you something about a distribution of _____. An | scores
average score or class average, for example, doesn't tell anything about the range, but it does tell you something else. Look at this figure.
The letters L and H stand for
the _____ score and | lowest
L—————H the _____ score, which | highest
determine the _____ of the distribution. | range

63. The range tells you something about the spread of the distribution, but tells you nothing about the class average on the test. The common arithmetical average of two scores, 10 and 14, is 12. To calculate this average, add 10 and 14, and divide by the number of scores. In this case the number of scores is only # _____ . $10 + 14 =$ | 2
_____ , divided by the number of scores | 24
is equal to # _____ . | 12

64. To find the average of these numbers—10, 11, 12, 15 and 17—you first _____ all the | add
numbers, and find their total to be # _____ . | 65
To find the average you then _____ this | divide
total by # _____ and find the average to | 5
be # _____ . | 13

65. To find the average of a set of scores you should
**_____.
_____
_____.

(Read frames 63 and 64 to find the correct answer.)

66. In statistics there are actually several kinds of averages. The kind of average you just worked out is called the mean. For these three numbers—10, 11 and 15—12 is the _____.

mean

67. Another name for the common arithmetical average is the _____. The sum of the scores divided by the number of scores is equal to the _____.

mean

mean

68. For this set of scores—8, 8, 10, 11, 11, and 12—the sum of scores is #_____ and the number of scores is #_____.

60
6

69. From the previous frame, if you divide 60 by 6, you find that the _____ is equal to #_____.

mean
10

70. 5, 5, 6, 7, 7, 7, 8, 8, 9, 10. For this set of scores the range is #_____ and the mean is #_____.

6
7.2

71. If you correctly indicated that the range was 6 in the last frame, skip to frame 74; but if you said that the range was either 5 or 10, go on to the next frame.

72. If you said that the range was 10, go on to the net frame; but if you said that the range was 5, look at these scores again: 5, 5, 6, 7, 7, 7, 8, 8, 9, 10. L = #_____ and H = #_____. In determining the range, it does not make any difference that 5 had a _____ of 2. The range—and you should have remembered this—is H − L + 1. In this case the range is equal to #_____ minus #_____ plus 1 equals #_____.
Now skip to frame 74.

5, 10

frequency

10, 5

6

73. You said that the range was equal to 10. That's wrong. There are 10 scores, but between the lowest score and the highest score, inclusive, there are only 6 *different* possible scores, 5, 6, 7, 8, 9, and 10. The range is $10 - 5 + 1$, which equals #_____.

6

74. One kind of statistical average is called the _____.

mean

75. A percentile, you remember, indicates the percentage of students who scored at or below a particular score. If a score of 36 is the 84th percentile, this means that **_____ _____ _____.

(See the second sentence in the next frame.)

76. On a test, 50 per cent of the scores fall at or below the *_____. If 36 is the 84th percentile, 84% of the scores were 36 or lower.

50th percentile

77. The 50th percentile can be thought of as the mid-point of a distribution. Another name for the mid-point is the median. The 50th percentile is the _____ or mid-point of a distribution.

median

78. The mid-point of a distribution is called the _____.

median

79. In this distribution—4, 5, 6, 7, 8—the median is 6. The median is defined as **_____ _____ _____.

(Frames 77 and 78 answer this question.)

80. The range tells you something about the ends of the distribution—the spread of scores between the _____ scores.

highest and lowest

81. The range tells you about the spread of the scores, while the mean and the median tell you something about the middle portion of the distribution. In a bell-shaped distribution the

scores tend to pile up—where? The answer appears in the first sentence, above. Underline the words that answer this question.

82. Because scores tend to pile up in the middle of a distribution, and because the mean and median are measures that are related to this tendency, the mean and median are called "measures of central tendency." The range, however, is not a measure of *_____ _____. | central tendency

83. The mean and the median are both called *_____. | measures of central tendency

84. Because both the mean and the _____ are found to lie near or at the middle of a set of scores, they are referred to as *_____ _____. | median / measures of central tendency

85. In addition to the median and the _____, there is a third measure of central tendency, and it is called the mode, which is simply the score with the highest frequency. If more students receive a score of 18 than any other score, then 18 is the _____. | mean / mode

86. The most frequent score is called the _____. | mode

87. The mean, median and _____ are all _____ of *_____. | mode / measures, central tendency

88. If a distribution of scores is perfectly bell-shaped, the mean, median and mode are all exactly the same, but if the bell is at all uneven or lopsided like this one, then the three measures of *_____ are all likely to be _____. | central tendency / different

The program would then proceed, following the type of construction that the programer had selected and which was found to achieve the objectives established for it. Obviously this is not a complete program—it is far too short to produce more than an elementary and introductory understanding of the concepts that were included. This sample program was tested on college students and on high school graduates who were not attending college. It was revised several times until very few errors were made while using the program, and until understanding of the content seemed to be adequate. A great many different kinds of frames were used in this brief program, and as far as could be determined, students did not tend to become distracted by the frequent changes in the program.

Index

125